INDIVIDUAL RESPECT IS A LANGUAGE EVERYONE CAN UNDERSTAND

INDIVIDUAL RESPECT IS A LANGUAGE EVERYONE CAN UNDERSTAND

Joe McNeill

INDIVIDUAL RESPECT IS A LANGUAGE
EVERYONE CAN UNDERSTAND

iUniverse books may be ordered through booksellers or by contacting:

iUniverse
1663 Liberty Drive
Bloomington, IN 47403
www.iuniverse.com
844-349-9409

Because of the dynamic nature of the Internet, any web addresses or links contained in this book may have changed since publication and may no longer be valid. The views expressed in this work are solely those of the author and do not necessarily reflect the views of the publisher, and the publisher hereby disclaims any responsibility for them.

Any people depicted in stock imagery provided by Getty Images are models, and such images are being used for illustrative purposes only. Certain stock imagery © Getty Images.

ISBN: 978-1-6632-1996-1 (sc)
ISBN: 978-1-6632-1997-8 (e)

Print information available on the last page.

iUniverse rev. date: 03/27/2021

For peace.

"When an old man dies, a library burns to the ground."
[An old African proverb.]

"I am an invisible man." Ralph Ellison

"no one is born hating someone because of the color of their skin." Nelson Mandela

"It is not a racial problem- it's a problem of whether or not you're willing to look at your life and be responsible for it- and then begin to change it. That great western house I come from is one house- and I am one of the children if that house. Simply I am the most despised child of that house- and it is because the American people are unable to face the fact that I am flesh of their flesh- bone of their bone- created by them. My blood- my father's blood- is in that soil." James Baldwin, Cambridge Debate, February 18th, 1965

"In the course of time there was a day that closed the last eyes to see Christ. The battle of Junin and the love of Helen each died with the death of some one man. What will die with me when I die, what pitiful or perishable form will the world lose? The voice of Macedonio Fernandez? The image of a roan horse on the vacant lot at Serrano and Charcas?

Jorge Luis Borges, From Dreamtigers, Translated by Mildred Boyer

Every single life has beauty, a uniqueness and validity, is irreplaceable- and is worthy of a basic human respect along with empathy and reciprocity.

Three social questions:

Do you want to be regarded and respected generally as the unique individual that you are by others or do you want to be judged principally and over-generalized by the color of your skin, your gender, religious affiliation, nationality, cultural association, or physical challenge?

What steps are necessary for that reality to happen generally for you and all your fellow individual human beings?

Is the path you are taking individually and socially following those steps that lead to that conclusion? Are the steps you are taking now leading away from that conclusion?

Three Elements of Peace:

To Recognize ourselves as exclusive, valid, unique individuals- as delineated from our culture or society- and the acceptance of the personal accountability that goes along with this recognition.

Empathy and identification with all other human beings as unique but fundamentally valid self-accountable fellow individuals like ourselves- putting ourselves in their shoes.

Behaving with a basic Reciprocity towards all others- treating all others the way we would want to be treated ourselves.

We can still be absolutely reverent to our religions, cultures, and countries as long as they don't stand in the way of, obscure, or subvert, a basic individual respect and priority of basic human rights between ourselves as fellow individual people together.

Can you identify with your ancestors of 60,000 years ago along with 500 or 10,000 years ago?

How well we do (and how our world does in this Anthropocene epoch) really comes down to individual human attitudes first and foremost. Individual attitudes can build a societal attitude.

If the above ideas were manifested in our classrooms, business cultures, public squares and places of worship- we would have more peace and less discrimination.

CONTENTS

ONE

//

First

No individual should have their skin color or gender define who they are throughout their lives on this planet. No person should feel forced to go through their lives defining themselves first and foremost socially as a member of a racial or gender group without their individual selves being recognized.

Honestly- we don't live in a world so much of cultural groups, religions, nations, skin colors, and genders as much as one of fellow individual people like ourselves. Recognizing your individuality and that of others is not the same as being individualistic- it is not selfish nor self-absorbed- not 'all about me'- it is instead our most widespread and fundamental common language and honest base of community with each other. The root of prejudice, terrorism, war and many of humankind's problems is a failure of people to recognize and accept their own individuality socially and respect and empathize with the fundamental individuality of all others. Socially we should recognize, empathize with, and respect each other as individuals regardless of what groups we belong to.

We need to transform into a 'fellow individual' based society rather than one of fundamentally separated groups of people. We can do this without losing our cultures, religions, nations, states, tribes, languages, etc. – we just need to prioritize- and lead with- individual respect towards all other people. We must create a reality in society where people are respected, empathized with, and treated with reciprocity as equal fellow individual people at a base level among each other. Individuality is a social condition that applies to everyone- therefore an ethic of individual respect applies to all of us regardless of our culture, language, religion, gender, nationality, etc.

In the near future there should be signs in the hallways of almost every school and business in America (followed eventually by the rest of our world) which say something to the effect of: "Individual Respect, Empathy, and Reciprocity is prioritized and practiced in this place. Individuals will not be discriminated against due to their skin color, gender, religious affiliation, physical challenge or sexual orientation."

Black, Gay, or deaf individuals in the near future will not automatically be thought of as principally Black, Gay or Deaf group members- but respected as fellow individual people who happen to have black skin, or who are gay, or who are deaf- and result will be an increased sense of community for those people rather than a decreased one.

None of us as human beings are exempt from the condition of being a unique individual among all others on this planet. No group, tribe, culture, people, nation, or even religion prevents us all from being fundamentally fellow individuals on a common level among all our other fellow individual people- and having an obligation to treat those people with a basic individual respect.

The primary social enemy of humankind is the idea and attitude that a specific group's culture makes us fundamentally who we are as individuals- and that this social group separates us fundamentally from all others who are not in our group. Too many of us are not recognizing ourselves individually and exploring our unique individuality (and the individuality of others) and instead are jumping into a separate tribal sense of esoteric group identity as a defense mechanism that is substitute for our primary identity. We find a sense of safety in numbers among "our good tribe" while comfortably relying on the notion that "the other tribes" are inherently bad or 'less than us'- which is seductive as an ironic means of self-preservation- hiding oneself in the group while group role-playing to protect oneself- and losing one's true self in the process.

Again- no individual should have their skin color or gender define who they are throughout their lives on this planet. No person should feel forced to go through their lives defining themselves first and foremost socially as a member of a racial or gender group without their individual selves being recognized.

This book asks what is the specific path for individuals who have black or brown skin or are female, or gay, or have a physical challenge, to live full lives free of prejudice and discrimination and the freedom to live without prejudice towards their fellow individual people- the freedom to be who they honestly can be.

To recognize ourselves and each other individually is not to ignore the reality of racial problems and unfairness- it is to give racial and gender injustice context that everyone can relate to- and the more people who can relate to and empathize with racial or gender injustice- the better. When a specific group is being treated unjustly those individuals have a right to- and must- defend themselves. Black people in America are forced to live through a system of disadvantage and unsafe situations with lethal consequences- simply because of their black skin. This is unacceptable in America and is absolutely contrary to our founding national creed that "ALL men are created equal".

Charles Blow's "The Devil You Know" (2021 Harper) argues that African Americans should return to the South in order to gain voting power to overcome the immediate threats facing individuals with black skin in this country- and this option unfortunately may be necessary for some time so that individuals can finally be recognized and respected as such- ironically by grouping together among people of the same skin color- but how will this lead to a world where people are truly free and respected individually without regard to the color of their skin? What is the path that their grandchildren will have to be accepted as individual people among others of all skin colors, genders, nationalities, religions, cultures, sexual orientations, physical challenges, etc.? The racist loves the idea of separated races- he says "I don't hate black people- they are just not *my* people- as long as *they* stay in *their* place and I have mine- everything is fine". It is a difficult dichotomy- where some of us feel forced to seek group protection for individual respect- but you and I will only be "free" when we can honestly define ourselves as the individual's we fundamentally are among all of our other fellow individual people and feel secure in that understanding and life condition.

Separate peoples are simply not going to work in the long term. A world where blacks live here and whites over there etc. is not a free world for individual people- for any of us. The only effective argument and defense against racism, bigotry and prejudice is the reality that we are not fundamentally different peoples- black, white, brown, male, female, etc.- that we should justly be treated as the fellow individual people that we actually are.

TWO

In Short

I f we really want to get down to the serious endeavor of increasing peace for humanity, preserving and fostering our natural habitat and the flora and fauna thereof, drastically decreasing the incidents and chances of war, terrorism, racism, bigotry, sexism, and increasing a socially healthy sense of community among human beings who live in different parts of our world who have not met each other, speak different languages, have different religions and cultures- this *can* be done.

Many of our human social conflicts are based on identity and how we classify ourselves and each other. A basic individual respect is self-evident between us as strangers who pass each other on an isolated beach or share a city elevator. As strangers our human instinct is to lead socially with a basic individual respect rather than culture- because a faint unspoken intuition reminds us that we *learned* our culture but a basic individual respect we *sense- and already remotely understand- is universal* and links us to others. The racist, bigot, or terrorist almost certainly envisions pleasant thoughts when they consider the phrase "these good people are enjoying themselves"- until the word "people" is suddenly substituted by a particular *group of people* that they don't like or feel they intrinsically don't agree with.

We are each alike- but not the same. The individual is the only social group, category or tribe that all human beings belong to equally. We, each and all, are intrinsically *fellow individual people* before we are Black, White, Brown, Female, Male, Christian, Muslim, Hutu, Tutsi, Israeli, Palestinian, Conservatives, Liberals, etc. We have no choice in this condition that we each find ourselves in. We do not get to choose or personally define who we fundamentally are among all others- because our individuality in social context is inescapable. If we can differentiate ourselves in even the slightest way from another person in our tribe, or culture, or on our planet- or even if we cannot- we are individuals socially simply as a condition of being alive. **We need the reality of distinct and valid individuals to experience love; there can be no love without an "other" to relate to.**

There is no inherent link between skin color and behavior or values or attitudes. There are no inherent social groups of human beings on our planet Earth who are separate from the rest of us. There are groups- and they may be very significant in many different ways- but all of the social groups that have ever existed are made up of valid individual people- such as we all are. Recognizing the reality of one's individuality among all others is not a call to selfishness or for one to be separate- it is instead our broadest and most inclusive common ground platform for community and can promote a sense of togetherness and cooperation. Unlike in an Ayn Rand novel (and nothing against Ayn Rand novels- some agreeable and disagreeable stuff there in my opinion)- the relationship of accepting the condition of one's individuality socially with the acceptance of the dominance of one's selfish ego are *not* linked. There is no inherent link between the words "individual" and "selfish". The former is a condition we all share, and the latter is a mindset. In fact, many behaviors that we consider selfish like ostentatious materialism (bling) are really conformity to perceived ideals of culture *away from* individuality and thinking independently. In reality- everyone equally shares our mutual condition of individuality socially and the only philosophical implication inherent in that condition is individual respect- no "selfish ego" is required. In society it is questionable whether it is in an individual's rational self-interest to be selfish. Without the concept of the individual there is no love, no empathy, no reciprocity, no respect, and no reverence. Thinking of ourselves as individuals teaches us that we could behave like our fellow individuals in any group- we are capable of that good or bad behavior or thought process- that these are not exclusive to certain groups or "peoples" only. It is esoteric group identity that most often leads to the separation of human beings while individual respect is all inclusive. "*We're all in this together* as fellow individual human beings"- is a more inclusive attitude than the *only* other alternative- that we are all fundamentally members of inherently separate groups destined to separate ourselves into a permanent state of cooperative pluralism at best.

All human beings, being individuals, are subject to a basic individually respective ethics underneath and across their religion, skin color, gender, culture, nationality, sexual orientation, etc. and being a world fundamentally socially of fellow individual people- the peace minded objective for all of us should be to foster a world where individuals are respected and treated fairly on this basic, common ground social level regardless of their skin color, gender, religion, nationality, sexual orientation, physical challenge, or culture. All good socially behaving people consider themselves- and all others- members of the "individually respective group" *before* considering themselves esoteric members of their cultural, or skin color, or religious, or national, or gender group, team, or tribe. Most of our world's religions involve individual choice as a critical component of the reverence and acceptance involved in that religion. The attitude of Loyalty to any group over individual respect - always only taking your group's side- without question and individual conscience "right or wrong"- means the downfall of all of us- together.

"Justice" is always what is just for an individual person among other individual people. There can be no honest justice if there is a separate standard for black or brown or white skinned individuals- for male or female individuals- for homosexual or straight individuals etc. The Individual must be the measuring standard for justice- especially in a society of racial, gender, cultural and religious biases. Since we are not all black, white, female, male, etc. but we are all individuals- we need one individual standard for justice that is applied fairly to each and all of us. This will never happen if we define ourselves intrinsically as white, black, female or male.

Culture is necessary and often wonderful, but people cause problems for themselves and the rest of society when they overlook or even deny their individual perspective and *live for* culture- as if their purpose in life is principally *to fit in to-* and *simply be a component of-* culture. Those who have "lived" this way their entire lives- never looking up or out from their culture- not recognizing or respecting their unique individual perspective- have arguably never been "alive" at all.

This is not a book designed to take up the important cause of explaining the black, white, brown, male or female perspective in an unjustly racially, or gender, divided and dominated society. Many books, plays, films, poems and songs already do a great job of this- and many more are needed. This book asks 3 questions relevant to every human being who lives among others:

1. Do you want to be regarded and respected generally as a unique individual by others or do you want to be judged principally and over-generalized by the color of your skin, gender, religious affiliation, nationality, cultural association, or physical challenge?

2. What steps are necessary for that reality to happen generally for you and all your fellow individual human beings?

3. Is the path you are taking individually and socially following those steps that lead to that conclusion? Are the steps you are taking now leading away from that conclusion?

What racism is- is not that black or brown skinned individuals are not being respected as black or brown people- but that they are not being included and respected and empathized with as fellow valid, holistic individual people. Our mutual problem is that many from the right and the left imagine an inevitable future world where groups are separated still- and the solution lies in changing these people's attitudes.

Our society will improve substantially with a decrease in war, terrorism, racism, bigotry, and sexism when we begin identifying and respecting people *first as individuals*- and as group members according to skin color, gender, religion, culture, or nationality- only afterwards. This individual emphasis is simply a condition of reality and existence- and our one honest base and common ground of community and love- among the rest of our fellow human beings. We are victimized by racism, bigotry, sexism when we are not honestly being respected as the valid individuals that we fundamentally are among all others. That valid individual person in each and all of us needs to be spoken for.

You and I and everyone else begin as individuals in our world and carry this fundamental identity with us throughout our lives. Not one of us should be overgeneralized as fundamentally black, white, brown, female, male, etc.- to do this is to show a lack of respect for the valid holistic person that we each are underneath our skin color or gender, culture, or religion. No one is victimized or unfairly discriminated against when they are treated as an equal individual. The common motivation of the 911 terrorists, the Apartheidists of South Africa, the Klan of Mississippi, the Hutu militias, the Nazis against the Jews was a perception that they were fundamentally members of a static group fighting against members of another fundamentally separate group with which they shared no relevant common connection as fellow individual people. They didn't define their victims as fundamentally fellow people *like themselves*. A perception of a world divided into fundamentally separate groups becomes *your* problem when it devolves into one of terrorism, sexism, hate, racism and bigotry towards you or eventually towards those you care about in our shared connected world. You may not face the direct discrimination- but you will eventually suffer in some way from the societal, or even global, crossfire.

What is best for individual people underneath and across any categorization of skin color, gender, religion, culture, sexual orientation etc. is the only just common ground for achieving social justice. We need to enjoy, celebrate, and learn from our various cultures, religions, nationalities, and macro diversity- but we also desperately need to integrate worldwide as the fellow individual people that we actually are- and recognize, celebrate, and benefit from our *individual diversity*- together.

So what do we need to do to foster the process of being individually recognized, empathized with, respected, and treated with reciprocity?

Please consider for a moment the levels of your identity- both how you perceive yourself and how others may perceive you. You have a gender, a skin color, a nationality, an acquired language, perhaps a religion and/or a cultural affiliation, and perhaps a bond of shared experience with a certain group of others along with which you may have experienced oppression, discrimination, war, generational events and generational mores, or some other experience. You may live through an environment that pressures you to define yourself generally by your skin color, or gender, or religion, or sexual orientation because of societal discrimination- or you may feel free to define yourself as whatever you like.

We all have various skin colors and genders and wear lenses of language, social mores, and culture (and many of us religion) over our individual point of perspective and exclusive individuality that filter our view of other people and the world around us- but each of us has a unique and valid consciousness, perspective and point of action which is different from any other human being. We may have gotten the false impression from our junior high school social studies class that the idea of the individual in society is a western civilization concept- but all human beings- even those who have no words in their language for 'me" or "I" are unique individual people. No two people share the exact same thoughts or memories or occupy the exact same physical space. We don't have a choice in being individuals in society. If you or anyone else can delineate you from anyone else in any way no matter how seemingly insignificant- you are an individual among the rest of us in our common world. This was the basis of the phrase "all men are created equal" in the American declaration of independence. We all share this social condition of exclusive individuality underneath all other levels of our identity- it is our point of action where our personal decisions to feel empathy and practice reciprocity, to be honest, to have integrity, to be bold in our curiosity and to strive intellectually, to not be corrupt, are made.

None of us is a member of any social group including religion, culture, tribe, gender, nationality, etc. to such an extent that we are not fundamentally a unique individual first and foremost among all other people socially. Not everyone is Catholic, Muslim, or French- but all Catholic people, Muslim people, and French people are individuals and when these same Catholic, Muslim and French people share an elevator, or an auditorium, or a planet- they are fundamentally, first and foremost, fellow individuals together and reciprocal individual rights take priority over cultural or religious differences.

If you want to be respected as the valid, unique individual person that you are- and you would like the same respect for other human beings- if you want a future world where individuals are not limited by their skin color, gender, religion, nationality, or culture in their pursuit of honesty, happiness, and goodwill towards other people and their environment- then we need to plan and follow steps that make this near future a reality.

We can begin by asking what is best for ourselves individually and our fellow individual people and the environment around us that sustains us, that we are a part of, and that we live in.

We need a true measurement for justice consistent across various groups of diverse peoples- we are all fundamentally individuals socially-this condition of being an individual is our common denominator- our common ground. A pluralistic world of diverse but fundamentally separate groups will never get us to individual respect and justice for everyone because none of us is a mere component of a racial, gender, religious, national, or cultural group. It is too easy to overlook or hide our valid individual selves underneath perceived groups of skin color or gender, tribe, religion, culture, nationality, etc. It is too easy to say and think "those Muslim- or White- or Latina- or Women- or Men- or homosexuals-*think that way*" while forgetting that the people in question being over generalized are valid individual people in their own right capable of having, learning, or changing independent thought and attitudes that are distinct from the stereotype of their religion, gender, sexual orientation, nationality, skin color, age, associated culture or generation, etc.

It is too easy to make demands of "society" as "rights" without considering the individual production and fair exchange necessary to make the products of those demands possible for ourselves or others. It takes the individual production, exchange and cooperation motivated by rational self-interest of individual people all over our globe to make a year's supply of pencils much less a computer or a respirator.

Our global society will improve in a myriad of ways if we recognize and respect the individual in ourselves and others and stop defining ourselves as fundamentally separate esoteric group members who we perceive are inherently apart from each other.

This condition of being an individual- among others who are our fellow individuals- is the common ground we all can learn to agree on- whether we are an Atheist, or born again Christian, or devout Muslim, or black, or white, or brown skinned, female or male, American, or Afghan etc. As you would like to be treated with at least a basic amount of individual respect from other people- so would everyone else- so our social goal should be a world that's good for individuals- a world where people are regarded and respected as the valid individual people that they really are.

Bad things happen when we don't recognize the individual in another person- when we don't treat the other person like we would like to be treated ourselves individually- and culture is most often the excuse for not doing this i.e. "women in our culture are traditionally treated this way" or "we must respect our tradition as a caste culture" or "they are just brown or black skinned people in a third world country and they don't matter as much as we do" or "that's just the way white people think" or simply the age old "We are in God's favor and that group of people is not".

Although we each learn to wear lenses of culture and socialize into certain groups, cultures, tribes, religions, languages, and nationalities that may appear to separate us from other human beings who seem to belong to different groups than we do- in reality we are fundamentally always fellow individuals first and foremost among all others regardless of our- or their-skin color, religion, gender, culture, tribe, nationality, language, or any other esoteric group. If we want peace for ourselves and others the worst thing we can do is lose track of, and respect for, our individual identity and the fundamental individual identity of all others. We are lost and become pawns for fostering unjust discrimination if we buy into the idea that we are fundamentally- *by definition*-at our core- White, or Latina, or Black, or Female, or Gay, or French or any other esoteric social grouping other than fundamentally an individual among all other individuals.

We are even fellow individuals first and foremost along with those who may oppress or discriminate against us because of our skin color, gender, religion, sexual orientation, or a physical challenge we may have, a nationality we belong to, or language that we speak. These oppressors often would like to categorize and define us as fundamentally group members of separate groups that they do not belong to and hope that we buy into the restriction of the definition of ourselves as fundamentally a member of a racial, gender, religious or cultural group with barriers that restrict our identity and growth potential. Just because these people define, and thus restrict, themselves into perceived racial, gender, cultural, religious, national or other separate boxes from their fellow human beings doesn't mean that we have to. Racist minded individuals want a world of fundamentally separate groups- and when we define ourselves or others as group members first according to skin color or gender or culture- we play into their world view or agenda. Be wary when a person of skin color A says of a person of skin color B "I have many friends of skin color B- they are wonderful people". Try asking person A if she considers those of skin color B "her people" as much as people of skin color A are......If it is evident that she does not- this is the basis of racism in our society- placing the definition of one by one's skin color above the definition of them as a fellow individual like ourselves.

When is it ok to over-generalize another fellow individual person because of their skin color or gender? When is ok to limit what they can explore artistically and tell them some musical styles are not for individuals of their skin color because the art belongs to another culture or skin color? Another challenge to an honest assessment of ourselves in society comes from those who teach young people to limit their view of themselves and other people to skin color, culture, and/or gender. They may teach young boys to be proud of their white skin and a pseudo "white heritage" or teach young girls who otherwise want to explore their individual identity to *define* themselves permanently as fundamentally brown skinned females in a predominantly white male racist world. The key word in the last sentence is "define". To be sure black or brown skinned people in America unfortunately need to consider, organize, and fight back against the outrageous and stupid state of oppression that is an unfortunate reality that they have been burdened with – but these brown skinned girl individuals should be *defining* themselves by the reality that they are fundamentally valid unique individual people, with unique perspectives to explore and share, who are living temporarily in a context where other individuals who temporarily have power are discriminating against them because of their skin color and gender. They should, as should all of us, insist on being recognized first and foremost not as brown skinned females but as the valid unique individual people that they in fact are- along with everyone else- in order to create a just world for themselves and all others. This definition of oneself as an individual among individuals underneath being white, black, brown, male, female, gay or straight etc. is so important and key to individual rights because it will be impossible to build a world where people are free among each other if people continue to define themselves fundamentally as white, black, brown, male or female, etc. A person who defines themselves by – and wants to permanently be regarded as- a member of a skin color, gender, tribe, nationality or culture apart from other human beings who do not share those attributes- will never be a free individual person among all others and may only perpetuate a world where people are not judged by the content of their character but by their gender or the color of their skin.

What is our goal for the betterment of fellow people of all skin colors and genders and cultures and religions, nationalities etc.? What type of future world do we want to live in? Do we want a world of individual respect for everyone where people are not overgeneralized and discriminated against by skin color, gender etc.? If so, our path needs to be one of individual respect first and foremost- a permanently pluralistic world of fundamentally separate groups without a bridge of individual respect connecting all underneath and across these groups that is being fostered by some right wing and left-wing attitudes will never get us there. The remedy for white individual oppression against black individuals is for white people to recognize black skinned people first and foremost as fundamentally fellow individual people like themselves- *their* fellow individual people. To define ourselves or others by our skin color, or gender, or nationality or even religion apart from other individuals who do not share the same affiliations is to deny *who we really are*- who *they really are*- hide from reality- and limit the lives and potential of ourselves and others. If we understand that every human being is worthy of individual respect then it is never ok to separate ourselves in our minds or actions as a member of a fundamentally separate group that they do not belong to. We can never be on the side of justice if we define ourselves as fundamentally separate from another fellow human being because of our skin color or culture or gender etc. - whether we are doing this as a white, black, brown skinned or male or female person this will never be consistent with social justice. True social justice is based on the recognition that every human being regardless of skin color or culture or gender etc. is a valid individual human being just as you are- and just as everyone is.

This last argument should not be confused with the right-wing argument that these brown skin girls have no inherent disadvantage in society because of their skin color or gender and should just pull themselves up by their bootstraps "just as white individuals do". All lives can't matter until black lives matter- and the response phrase "all lives matter" has been used by too many to refute the reality that black skinned individuals have had to face a particular disadvantage, racism, and existential threat simply due to their black skin in our society that should be one of fellow individual people treated equally. In a society of predominantly white skinned people- it is often, and has most often been, easier for white skinned individuals to be recognized, and have the freedom to live their lives, as unique individuals with individual opportunity in society. It is sad that some young black mothers have felt compelled to move with their children to all black environments ironically so their children may be recognized as the unique individuals they are and pursue individual perspectives, insights and opportunities denied them in social environments of stereotyping and overgeneralization. An increase in the attitudes of more and more people that we should live in a world more so of individual respect and a decrease in the attitude that people can be generalized as group members according to race, gender, culture, religion, etc. is the solution to this problem.

A vision of the future where people are defined and separated according to skin color, gender, culture or religion is a restricted one in which people have still not learned- or grown the courage to accept- the reality that all people are fellow individuals first and foremost socially.

THREE

//

The Why and How

This book is addressed primarily to young people. When I was younger this is the perspective I would have liked to have been exposed to while I was learning of and exploring the existing established waves of thought of religion, conservatism, liberalism, racism, feminism, libertarianism, objectivism, etc.

Human beings have many social problems because many of us don't delineate ourselves from- and instead define ourselves by- culture. Culture is important and can be wonderful but we must not socialize into it to the extent that we view ourselves as fundamentally separate group-wise from our fellow individual human beings outside the confines of our various cultures. We must not become "cultural robots" living our "lives" on cultural autopilot.

So many books and educational material dealing with racism, bigotry and prejudice seem to begin with the prejudicial premise that people are fundamentally White, Black, Latina, Male, or Female- instead of being fundamentally individuals first among each other. Given the legacy and outrageous current reality of societal group separation and relative advantage/disadvantage according to skin color, gender, etc. this is understandable- but it is not reality. It is simply not true that any human being is inherently or fundamentally White, Black, Latina, Homosexual, Male or Female- despite the reality of the persistent unjust prejudice and/or discrimination against individuals who have these or other attributes. The fact that an individual has been consistently confronted with the reality of the significance of their skin color, gender, or sexual orientation in the minds of other people or the system they are forced to inhabit should never overshadow the reality of their validity as a unique individual among all others. The reality is that we all begin the same as individuals first- before we learn to separate ourselves and assign meaning to social groups that we feel we or others may, or may not, belong to. Defining oneself as a member of a culture, system, or cause can lead people to (often unwittingly) prioritize disrespect over individual respect, empathy, and reciprocity. As an individual or a member of a tribe, culture, nation, skin color, or gender we cannot run or hide away from the rest of the individuals in our world. All other people are fundamentally *your people* on our shared planet- all individual life has a unique valid perspective just as you do.

As a college student years ago I remember that in discussions of race I didn't encounter even one self-identified white skinned liberal or democrat person who didn't regard themselves as a fundamentally white person who would love to help increase equality of opportunity for black or Hispanic people- who- in their eyes- were *fundamentally black or fundamentally Hispanic*. One particular person, when referring to a group in the middle east, actually said "they don't really have individuals over there- those people have been living that way for thousands of years" (!). These people had socialized into their perception of culture to the extreme extent that they actually felt defined and bound by what should have been a very real but permeable abstraction. Those fellow students of mine who felt that "there is a certain way that white, or black, or Latino people think" were overlooking the possibility that an individual who is white or black or Latino could think primarily for themselves- and the fact that all of us are- in reality (although many times we pretend not to be)- unique thinking individuals. Did these people really believe that fixed general attitudes or behaviors come with a skin color? I remember being frustrated that we were in trouble as a society and a planet if we didn't recognize and identify with others as fundamentally individual people like ourselves first before considering and dealing with the pluralistic world of groups we inhabit together. I remember processing the inescapable logic that Martin Luther King's dream of "one day where all are judged not by the color of their skin but by the content of their character" would be impossible if individual people continue defining themselves and each other as not only white or male- but black, brown, female or inherent members of a particular culture as well.

Because of our "all men are created equal" founding national creed - the measure of how well America is living up to its promise is to a large extent the measure of how well Black people, Women, Hispanic Americans, Asian Americans, Native Americans, and other Non-White Male Americans are doing. The struggle of Women, Native American, Black, Latino, and Homosexual individuals *is the American story-* one of individuals who must struggle against repression because of an un-asked for attribute that one has- and dealing with the affiliation one has with others who are discriminated against because of the same attribute. Frederick Douglass, Thurgood Marshall, Medgar Evers, Lorraine Hansberry and Martin Luther King lived and fought through the American experiment of individual struggle and opportunity as much if not more so than Adams, Jefferson, Madison, Washington, Paine and Franklin. The black skinned man Crispus Attucks was the first American to give his life for the American Revolution. Two hundred fifty Years earlier the first explorer to lead Europeans into what would later become the western United States was the black man Mustafa Azemmouri (who also gave his life in that exploration). If women or black people were fairly integrated in the 18th century according to the principles of our Declaration of Independence then we would certainly not have the huge disparities and cultural delineations in race and gender that we have now. Even though it often seems to some white people that there is a major constant disproportionate focus on people of color in in American culture- in fact America needs to do this to keep measuring ourselves to our declaration's founding American values. This is the way we measure our American experiment of individual liberty: looking at and measuring our fellow individual people and/or individual Americans and asking ourselves "are my fellow individual people being treated fairly- as I would like to be treated?"- and reinforcing the attitude that if women, Native Americans, black, Latina, or homosexual people are *fundamentally my fellow individual people* deserving individual rights then *their struggle is my problem and my concern.*

I also remember wanting to ask those who define themselves or others as white, black, Latina, male or female "how will this definition of yourself lead to your liberation among others honestly as a fellow individual?" and "when will be the day in the future when this definition of yours leads to a social world of free individual people?" Of course, the answer is that it never can and never will. Change in the future doesn't happen without ideals, a vision, a focal point goal, and attitudes to get there. If we want a world where people are judged predominantly by the content of their character and not by skin color then we need to drop the mindset of a future strictly pluralistic world of fundamentally White people coexisting with fundamentally Black people (or Latin people, Female people, German people, etc.) We need to become a world of Fellow Individual people first and foremost socially- and group members of race, ethnicity, gender, religion, nationality or culture only afterward. Have the honesty and courage to tell your culture "no" when it leads you away from individual respect. You shouldn't feel forced to live your life *for* culture- no one should. Among other people our social obligations, priorities and allegiances are individual respect first socially before cultural, religious, or political *practices* (not necessarily beliefs). A fundamentally pluralistic world of separate groups accordingly skin color, culture or even religion is not ok and not realistic.

We live in a world now in which the rampant racism, bigotry, prejudice, sexism, group advantages/disadvantages need to be identified, confronted, and remedied and there are many fronts that rightly highlight these problems by focusing on the groups involved- however this book is an attempt to remind all of the inescapable logic that ultimately a pluralistic world of fundamentally separate groups will never be one in which individual people are honestly free to explore their own unique potential and share in the wonderful and productive individual diversity of others. To experience love is to experience difference- and share the wonderful individual perspectives, uniqueness and diversity among ourselves together.

People adopt bad individually dis-respective attitudes (attitudes towards climate change denial, white nationalism, religious persecution, racism, prejudice, jingoism, sexism, homophobia, etc.) from their desire to belong to culture or the cultural component of religion (one of the strongest forms of culture)- which can sometimes lead to a mindset that there are fundamentally different separate groups of people in our world and that individuals are, or can be, mere components of those groups. It is generally the attitudes of individuals that are the problem and the solution to so many of our world's shared challenges as fellow human beings as we evolve to be better people.

When we walk out into our world as individuals and begin to encounter others- be they family, tribal, religious or cultural members that we feel an affiliation with or others we encounter in our cities and countries that we feel a bit less connected to or still others in far-away lands of completely different languages, cultures, religions or social contexts- we should remember that they are all individuals like us who began like us with whom we can share the universal common language of individual respect including empathy and reciprocity- together peacefully.

FOUR

///

Liberation

O ur individuality and the implications of individual respect that logically follow come before we learn anything about religion or culture or the language of ourselves or anyone else- even before the absolute significance of our family, our tribe or our country- as humans before the profound relevance to us of the meaning of Black Lives Matter or Slavery or White Privilege or Wounded Knee or the Ghost Dance or Ponte Du Hoc.

All human beings are born unique valid individuals before we learn of, or become knowing members of, anything else- including any language, history, heritage, culture or religion. Since we all share this condition of individuality in common- individual respect always should come before cultural or religious *practice* (although not necessarily cultural or religious *belief*) *if* the religious or cultural practice conflicts with a basic individual respect among ourselves.

We can still respect our religions, our cultures, our countries, and our social conditions but we should never violate a fundamental individual recognition/respect, empathy and reciprocity for our fellow human beings underneath and across all other layers of ourselves socially. Every one of us is an individual- not every one of us shares the same religion, culture, gender, skin color, sexual orientation, language, nationality, etc. Our individuality is our common ground- among ourselves- together.

A world of generally free interacting individual people where a basic individual respect is the common practice would be best for everybody (each and all of us as human beings) but we can never get there if people keep *defining themselves* by their skin color, esoteric culture, nationality, gender, or even religious group- *apart* from the rest of our human family. This is a major challenge in a reality where some groups may be socially dominant and in a position of inherent and disproportionate power and social advantage- such as white skinned male individuals in a certain social context- and black or brown skinned female individuals sharing that same context. It may be much harder for the latter to be respected as individuals and regard themselves as individuals than the former- simply because of an unfair social environment they were born into. The abhorrent social condition in which the latter above individuals find themselves no doubt necessitates recognizing the social group dynamics involved and resisting the injustice as a group- but they lose much more if they accept in themselves the unreality and lie that they are not fundamentally valid unique individuals- just as valid individually as any other human being- including fellow individuals of another skin color, gender, sexual orientation, religion, or culture who just happen temporarily to be in power in the moment. A malevolent racist or sexist minded individual wins a terrible victory when they convince the subject of their racism or sexism that the former is the default normal human being while the subject is the inherent member of an inferior group separate from the valid whole. The racist or sexist behaving individual is illuminated in the light of justice when the subject individual believes and can confidently (and lawfully) declare to the oppressor: "I'm every bit the valid individual human being worthy of basic individual respect that you are and my race, ethnicity, gender, religion, nationality, sexual orientation or culture has nothing to do with that fact".

The dominant attitudes of the general population regulate the behavior of people in any society or shared planet. We need to teach, promote and foster fundamental social attitudes of individual respect among our young people now. Specifically:

1. the Recognition of ourselves as exclusive, valid, unique individuals as delineated from our culture or society and the acceptance of the personal accountability that goes along with this recognition.
2. Empathy and identification with all other human beings as unique but fundamentally valid self-accountable fellow individuals like ourselves.
3. behaving with a basic Reciprocity towards all others.

This Recognition, Empathy, and Reciprocity will be abbreviated in this book as RER. If our goal is to get to a near future where all people are recognized respected judged as the valid individual people they are rather than over-generalized by skin color or gender etc.- we need RER-like values to be honored and expected in our schools and businesses.

What stands in the way for most of us in recognizing ourselves, empathizing with others as fellow individuals, and treating others with reciprocity is Culture. It is culture that keep can keep us from seeing a fellow human being first and instead see black or white skin first or gender or a religious affiliation first.

The enemy is not usually culture itself but *the defining of oneself by one's culture*- and our social problems are not usually due to people themselves but their attitudes- and attitudes for most people can change. In many cases we can blame the attitudes of individuals defining themselves by- and going along with- culture for such things as cigarette smoking, climate change denial, bigotry, prejudice, xenophobia, believing propaganda or conspiracy theories, poor diet, unhealthy choices, drug addiction, a money centric-above-all-else lifestyle, religious or cultural dogma that doesn't respect others or leave space for individual views, a cultural narrowmindedness towards music or art that one is not used to, terrorism, gun violence, gang violence, institutional corruption that may occur in the workplace, unions, police forces or governments- or even just not questioning culture itself- all these could be reduced if we prioritized individual respect, empathy and reciprocity if these conflict with a culture that we feel we belong to.

Our future will be better for us all if we foster RER among each other- especially in our schools and workplaces. Just as the "We are an equal opportunity employer" signs were prevalent in the entrances of large companies in the late 20th century we should have voluntary ubiquitous declarations in our schools and businesses that say (*and mean it*) **"We are an Individually Respective school (*and/or business*)"**. Such declarations would announce and set the tone for a baseline behavior of individual respect (individual recognition, empathy and reciprocity) for *all* who enter underneath and across any social category or designation of race, ethnicity, gender, religion, nationality, culture, physical challenge or sexual orientation.

FIVE

The Logic to Peace

There is an achievable logic to peace- and to also generally feeling good about ourselves socially, our fellow human beings, our impact on the environment around us and our place in the context of the unique and exclusive life that we each journey through. Social attitudes like the following need to be considered and acted on if we are to improve our world together:

1. We are, each and all, fundamentally unique individuals among each other and all other people- never members of a separate culture or separate religion which is fundamentally apart from any other human being.

On our own we can define ourselves as whatever we like- but once we step into the company of others we have no choice but to become fundamentally unique self-accountable individual persons among all others- distinct from the tribes that we may feel that we belong to. Our culture does not make us fundamentally who we are- it has never made anyone fundamentally who they are. You were a valid human being before you learned about your language, tribe, culture, or religion- and you remain a valid human being to this day distinct from these. You do not necessarily need to look to your culture, ancestry, or religion to value and recognize your unique validity and personal accountability- or to value any other human being individually. We do not need to know what a stranger's background or culture is to give them individual respect.

Before any of us is a member of any group that may have been around for hundreds or even thousands of years- we are fellow individuals first among all other fellow human beings. All human beings begin the same as fellow members of a common tribe of individual people before we learn to separate ourselves according to language, culture, or religion. Recognizing and accepting that you are an individual point of perspective and accountability is essential before you can be honest with yourself, your interpretation of God, or anyone else. What we look like or the context that we were born into is only a tiny part of who we are- and although we may be judged and discriminated against based on appearances- we are always a valid, accountable individual before we are a member of any racial, ethnic, gender, religious, national or cultural group. Because we are rewarded or discriminated against according to these labels is no reason to define ourselves as something more general than who we honestly uniquely are.

2. Among all others- we must always prioritize individual respect and reciprocity.

We can conform to cultural norms and expectations- but always after we meet our obligations to all others on an individually respective level. There are no inherent human groups on our planet that are separate from any other perceived groups according to race, gender, culture, religion, nationality, or tribe. First and foremost, socially we are all fundamentally individuals living together. These truths are really self-evident to each of us even if buried under the warmth or scars of tribal affiliation. Groups are always made up of valid individual people like yourself. When you hear someone say "those liberals or right wingers always do this or think that way" it's certainly an exaggeration. In reality, it is individuals who are people just like you that act- not groups. We are all born with an individual obligation to treat all others with a primary individual respect and reciprocity- regardless if they belong to a group we belong to or not- such as skin color, gender, culture, language, religion, nationality, sexual orientation, etc. We are behaving morally if we do this- we are not behaving morally if we do not. If we don't treat people individually and institutionally the way we ourselves want to be treated then our society can't possibly get better. Politically we need to see our world as fellow individuals with individual human rights first before citizens of countries, members of race, or culture, or gender etc. Every child deserves to grow up in a world where they are not discriminated against for attributes they did not create such as their skin color, gender, or sexual orientation. None of us are born knowing what the significance of our skin color or gender etc. will be in the society we are born into. We are all born 100% unique individual in our world and 0% black, white, female, male, Japanese or Baptist, socially. Have the courage to be the individual that you really are underneath your culture and to recognize the individual first in everyone else regardless of skin color, gender, culture, nationality, religious association, etc. This is not to say that skin color doesn't matter- color has meant- and still means- everything- it just *shouldn't* mean everything. Color matters in America in that our core foundation is all men are created equal and the struggle of Black, Brown, Female, Native American and Gay people here is the real story of that premise challenge.

The parts of individual respect are self-recognition (delineating- but not necessarily separating- oneself from one's culture) personal accountability (honestly holding oneself to account) empathy with our fellow individual people and reciprocity. We each have an inherent obligation to recognize our individual personal accountability among all others. We should identify and empathize with other individuals concerning the contexts that they must deal with that may be different than ours and thus- in a sense- try to put ourselves in their shoes.

We should respect all others individually and always prioritize individual respect even if it conflicts with our perception of culture or religion. Culture or religion do not exempt us from our personal accountability among all other human beings or from the environment that we live in.

We should treat all others the way we would like to be treated ourselves individually. While it may at times be easier for us to group identify ourselves apart from others- prejudice comes from insecurity in not recognizing that we are individuals fundamentally just as all others are. We should always keep in mind that all others around us- even those we feel we know and love- are somewhat like the stranger approaching us from a distance and carry unique perspectives and are worthy of a certain amount of basic individual respect- as we would want for ourselves.

Individual respect and reciprocity are the social common ground platform that we all can base ourselves on underneath and across culture, religion, race, gender, and nationality- while still keeping these affiliations. Because we are all individuals- we must prioritize individual reciprocity among ourselves- even, and especially, if this is being impeded by cultural or religious disregard of individual respect. You want people who are now disagreeing with you to eventually agree with you. You want them to voluntarily change and have better social attitudes. Individual respect is our common language, our common bridge of connection and communication- our means of progress- it is everyone's common territory beneath perceived barriers of culture, tribe, religion, etc.

3. Culture- though important, wonderful, and even necessary- has never made you or I or any human being fundamentally and intrinsically who they are.

Culture at its worst can get in the way of us recognizing ourselves and our fellow human beings as people like ourselves and anesthetize us from recognizing individual respect and reciprocity. It takes honesty and courage to look past our culture and deal with certain individual realities.

It's individual allegiance to culture that is the root of so many of our social problems where individual respect is really the answer. Opposition to addressing climate change is allegiance to culture- opposition to women's and gay individual rights comes from allegiance to culture. Slavery in America and elsewhere has attempted to be justified by allegiance to culture and tradition. Many can reject the importance of individual production and exchange of themselves or others in favor of believing that somehow the culture they inhabit will just assert a will of its own where their personal action is irrelevant.

A great benefit of recognizing ourselves socially is that having a clean conscience in that we are being honest with who we are. Individual respect is relevant to you regardless of what esoteric group you belong to. To deny individual respect is to deny yourself and the core reality of your fellow human beings. It is not natural for culture to dominate humans or to turn over one's identity to culture while denying or losing track of our individual identity. Culture can be an anesthetic to certain realities that we should face and deal with. We can evolve ourselves socially past some of the negative side effects of culture and greatly reduce prejudice, war, poisoning our earth or killing off species that we share our planet with for the sake of cultural conformity.

Individuals generally don't want war and they can feel linked as fellow individuals with individual rights and empathy and deny wars that affect them started by esoteric powers who claim to represent esoteric groups of people. Individual rights do not have racial, gender, religious, cultural, or political boundaries. Any person of any skin color is capable of any attitude or behavior. Individual Chinese can be linked with individual Americans and individual Israelis can feel linked to individual Palestinians because they each value a priority of individual rights and what is right and good for individual people. Together they can deny war to the authorities above them that may want social discord among ourselves.

Culture can often keep us preoccupied from living our own lives and sharing who we really are with others. We can ignore the reality of our individual interacting world to conform to culture- and by doing this we roleplay socially on cultural autopilot rather than living our own honest lives with each other. To love someone else involves honestly sharing individual differences and perspectives. A "life" lived on cultural or religious dogma autopilot without the examination of one's own life and context or the consideration of the valid individual lives of other fellow human beings is an unlived life. Cultures and traditions can grow out of individual control and end up dominating individual lives. Some people "live" their entire life on cultural autopilot. We need to be careful about growing so accustomed to a "way of life" that we want to preserve it at the expense of ourselves or others growing individually. When something sublimely wonderful or terrible happens one who cares deeply about it often says the phrase "there are no words". This means words in our limited vocabulary or culture is glaringly limited when confronted with profound reality. We are so used to confining our world within our cultural reference that we may feel a connection to a profound reality outside and independent of our esoteric cultures but we have a hard time expressing it. Peeking our head outside of culture into the real unconstructed world around us can help all of us.

We need to move away from the perception that "that person over there" is simply a component of a people who "have lived that way for thousands of years". We spend too much time and energy relating to culture and not enough relating as fellow individual people. It takes courage to face our world with individual identity and recognize and respect the individual identity of all others and not fall into the oftentimes easier path of grouping and defining oneself and others by culture, religion, nationality, race, gender, sexual orientation etc. We will continue to have social problems of war, racism, prejudice, and terrorism until most people begin to view themselves and others as 99% unique individual and only 1% race, gender, culture, religion, etc. among all other people. Prejudice comes from people defining themselves and others by culture rather than as individuals.

Instead of seeing static foreign groups of refugees and immigrants as Hondurans, Syrians, Irish, Vietnamese or Jews why not face the reality that they are actually fellow individuals like ourselves but caught in different social contexts. We may someday achieve all individuals valuing individual rights, respect and empathy, so we may improve ourselves and our common circumstances together. We can share our individual lives together socially with common respect and still learn from and enjoy each other's cultures. We need more of the attitude that "that person *could be* me" and less "I'm just glad *that's not me*" to improve our shared social world.

4. The recognition of our valid individuality among each other does not mean that we must give up a sense of culture or religion or identity with certain groups- just that we should never forget the reality that we are all fundamentally fellow individuals together with all other people. When culture or religion interfere with individual rights and respect- we should always prioritize individual rights and respect.

The concept of Individual respect/reciprocity is our most common base rule, law, and path for conflict resolution among ourselves as human beings. We need to have the courage to be honest about who we are and be ok with ourselves and who others are individually. There is a valid Black in America perspective, a Latina perspective, a White male perspective, a Woman's perspective etc.- but a black person, Latina person, white male person and a female person deserve to be recognized and respected individually- distinct from how they may broadly define themselves or how others may overgeneralize them.

Joe McNeill

Cultural diversity is great except when it inhibits individual growth and inhibits a sense of fundamental brotherhood among human beings. There is no such thing as a human being who can be defined fundamentally as not an individual but a part of a "people" who have been living "that way" for thousands of years. There is certainly no behavior or attitude that describes individuals of any skin color. We as individual people can each become slaves to our cultures when we over-generalize other perceived groups of people as "fundamentally not like us".

5. We live in a world honestly of individuals- but ostensibly in a world of separate tribal groups- and the prejudice, racism, and discrimination between and among many of these groups is very real.

It is not easy for many to live as free expressive individuals as it is for others of a more socially favored skin color, gender or sexual orientation. Some American conservatives have overlooked the fact that white skinned male Christian individuals often begin their individual journey with social advantages that other equally valid individuals in society have not had- and yet have complained that these disadvantaged individuals should just "pull themselves up by their bootstraps" when they themselves didn't have to. It is important to acknowledge and empathize with what it must be like to face discrimination and stereotyping every day and how that understandably may enhance identity with a discriminated group- yet still stick up for the more primary individual in that person facing discrimination- and understand that defining oneself holistically as black or white or Latina or female will never lead to a world where people are not discriminated against due to a perception of being fundamentally black, white, Latina, or female. It is obvious that skin color privilege, cultural privilege, and social advantage such as white privilege and male privilege dominate in much of our world. We should be aware of social advantage and/or bias according to race, ethnicity, gender, religion, sexual orientation, nationality and/or culture in society as an existing threat against individual freedom. We must work so that no individual is overgeneralized, judged, or discriminated against because of a skin color, gender, sexual orientation or social disadvantage that they themselves had no part in creating. Because we are all individuals- any violation of someone else's individual rights is a violation of our individual rights. Those individuals "over there" are our people. Those people in Selma, Aleppo, Tian'amen Square, Auschwitz, Soweto, Juarez, Amritsar, Sand Creek, the MeToo movement, Stonewall, Lexington and Concord are *our people*. You have the power to reevaluate who "your people" are so that the attitude of "my people are only people of my culture"- can be reduced and your sense of community can be increased.

6. Individuals are distinct from, and can change, attitudes. It is social attitudes that are bad or good- and ideals that are great or not great- not individuals.

Attitudes and values do not come with a skin color- these things come from individual questioning and awareness or from culture. The three most important attitudes that should always come first before considering culture, skin color, gender, or even religious social practice in society are individual respect, empathy and reciprocity. These attitudes are relevant to every person, are self-evident, and can be easily understood by individuals generally underneath and across any cultural references. We humans are imperfect beings who are susceptible to dis-respective behavior towards ourselves, others or our natural environment. In our current Anthropocene epoch of unprecedented human influence on our planet- what will make our world better is when human beings behave better on a large scale- having individually respective attitudes and ideals. There are no black skin or white skin attitudes. There are cultures made up of individual people who choose attitudes or have attitudes pushed unto them. An attitude is way of thinking that affects a person's behavior. Ideals are a standard of perfection; a principle to be aimed at. Culture is the esoteric group behavior and norms created by humans found in human societies. Individuals are imperfect and beneath ideals- and the ideal of Individual Respect among everyone should always be above culture. A group cannot think only an individual can. Individual respect should be a paramount attitude socially even if it conflicts with the culture that you are comfortable with- even through the cultures that may dominate us like our cultural tribes, our jobs and the social roles we play in society. This is a fundamental respect for life. We may learn to like each other more- learning to value each other's reality- based on individuality rather than just cultural expectations and measurements.

Ideals last longer than individual human lives or esoteric cultures- and yet they arise and are perpetuated by the interactions of individual people. We need individually respective attitudes to prevail in our world and disrespectful attitudes to go away. Certain civilizations may have destroyed themselves because they were all about the rulers instead of ideals. It is more sustainable to live for ideals and keep evolving as living, thinking, decision making beings who respect each other and cooperate for mutual benefit. Good ideals continue while individuals are temporary so when one individual dies many others now can pick up and further the cause- and enjoy the benefits.

We fellow individuals are imperfect people (constantly changing "verbs") that can feel good about and improve ourselves through following ideals that are perfect. Soldiering peacefully through our short temporary lives we can further the conduit of increased peace and goodness and help evolve ourselves into better future beings.

Improving our world is about good social attitudes winning out among the general public over bad ones. Good ones are individually respective and bad ones are not.

7. Individual production and exchange in markets is humanity's natural biological mechanism for sustaining ourselves as a species.

You didn't earn the skin color, gender, or financial circumstances you were born into and neither did anyone else. As individuals we generally have only 5 choices for survival among each other. 1. We can try to produce everything we need by ourselves alone, 2. We can steal the production of others, 3. We can rely on the charity of others, 4. We can speculate by buying and then selling for a profit Land, Stocks, Homes, or other things of perceived value, or 5. We can examine ourselves and produce what we can individually and exchange this production with others.

Number one is problematic unless we can make our own cell phones, electricity, healthcare etc. by ourselves- and even if we could -the process of creating everything we need or want would take up most of our time in life. Number two depends on others producing, is probably not sustainable in the long run without harsh consequences and adversely affects our fellow individual people. Number three is, well... good luck with that. Number four is a form of gambling and since the only tangible gain is profit above everything else- this cold pursuit of profit in-itself may disregard other important factors in our human lives such as our natural environment (clean air, clean oceans, wildlife and ecosystems), the wellbeing and even safety of workers in industry, and the loss of jobs and homes of people without power who are affected by the far away transactions of other people's speculations, profits or losses.

Number five is the natural biological process human beings are adapted for to produce for themselves and others. We don't have the evolutionary advantages of big teeth and claws- we produce something through an individual aptitude we have or learn, and we exchange this production with other humans to sustain ourselves and each other. We find time and resources in our lives to produce what we can for others- while others do the same for us.

8. The profit based free market doesn't directly provide all that individuals need. As individuals living together- we need government, laws and rules- and the laws that apply to all of us should be justly based on how each of us would like to be treated individually through reciprocity.

Capitalism needs government in order to benefit society effectively. One element of government is to not consistently reward able-bodied individuals for not doing what they can to produce for themselves- but if the profit motive worked for educating all of a country's school children or for insuring pre-existing conditions- we wouldn't have these problems that have been persistent since long ago. It is the role of government to fill these needs where the profit motive doesn't exist. And the people who pay taxes have a patriotic duty to honor their obligations which is the price for them to live in society.

Individuals can get swept up in cultural waves and networks that hedge outcomes. Individuals begin at different starting points. There are always exceptions, but generally Beverly Hills kids do better educationally (access wise) and economically than Watts kids.

The role of Government is to secure justice and promote the general welfare of all individuals within a certain jurisdiction. All individuals being equal before the law regardless of social advantage or disadvantage is the basis of "All men are created equal" in the American Declaration of Independence, the basis of social justice, and all just laws and government. Governments role is how is *everyone* doing. Are some systematically disadvantaged? Who have market forces left behind? We need government because the free market rewards profit above our natural environment and everything else- and we don't always act with reciprocity ourselves. In a wild west environment without law- cheating, thugs and brute force will rule. If we left the private sector alone without government- we would still have slavery, child labor, death smog fogs in London and Pittsburgh, black codes, restricted hotels, etc. Until we achieve a world in which all individuals practice reciprocity some will steal from or harm others, pollute our shared natural environment for profit, and hedge social advantages for themselves at the expense of others who have less power. In a laissez faire environment it's relatively easy to make money in a market at the expense of others if you turn off your conscience. The achievement is to earn with integrity and not with unearned advantage or at the expense of resources you didn't create such as our natural environment. We need to get rid of the attitude that cheating, networking and referral without regard for merit, or grabbing the biscuit off the table without consideration of anyone else is somehow "hustle" and a good thing- it is not- it is weak and makes ourselves and our society weak.

Human beings are born with an obligation to individual respect and reciprocity. Every individual is obligated to a basic respect of the validity of every other individual they encounter. No individual is above this obligation (whether they be a monarch, a religious figure, a government official, or anyone else).

Individual production and exchange is the greatest tool mankind has ever known- and the most subversive force in liberating the individual in all of us from the overt control of an oppressive culture or dictatorship- but it has also led to a social environment where some are born on 2nd base economically with tremendous advantages while many other individuals through no fault of their own can't even get into the ballpark. The role of government is to promote the general welfare of, and fairness for, all individuals within a certain jurisdiction- and to carry out those necessities that may not be best provided for by the profit driven private sector such as individual access to common defense, education, healthcare and food and shelter for the poor. Government's job is to protect the consumer while business people need laws and government to set the boundaries of what they can do to achieve profit.

The reason we don't govern based on culture or religion is that culture and religion don't always place individual respect first and we're all individuals first among each other and all others. "All men are created equal" must apply to all people of any race, tribe, gender, religion, culture, sexual orientation or physical disability or it will have no meaning within any jurisdiction. Any just government is concerned with prioritizing individual rights and this is why we have federal over state jurisdiction in the U.S. because states may prioritize local culture over individuals. They may place local majority rule over the individual rights that should be protected for each and all of us- and black codes may still be in Mississippi and Alabama. When individuals are caught in traps of generational poverty with tremendous disadvantages in opportunity and access to education, healthcare, and living conditions- it is the duty of any just government of people who value reciprocity and individual success to help. One cannot be an advocate of individual rights if they don't empathize and put themselves in the shoes of other fellow individual people who have a disadvantaged social context.

All individuals need access to a reasonably safe environment free of unfair discrimination as well as access to affordable healthcare and education if at all possible. The profit market alone can allow the advantaged leverage where other individuals don't have the freedom to choose healthcare because it is unaffordable to them. If some individuals cannot get comprehensive health insurance that they can afford or if education is unaffordable then it is the role of government to promote the general welfare of individuals in the aggregate when the private sector market leaves them behind.

9. Honesty about our identity without overgeneralizing ourselves to each other allows for empathy, a greater sense of community, cooperation and love between ourselves.

Many of us live our lives in danger of becoming cultural robots. A lonely world where people fence themselves apart from each other while roleplaying to culture in the extreme can become one of cultural robots on autopilot rather than fellow human beings respecting the uniqueness of each other to exchange, learn, cooperate, love, and grow. It can be revelatory for you sometimes to imagine yourself at the end if your life looking back. How would you have wanted to live your life in relation to others and your environment?

10. Humanity can construct a world- in the near future- where people are judged not by their race, ethnicity, gender, religion, nationality or culture but by the content of their individual character, graduating from fundamental attitudes of cultural diversity to individual diversity.

You must state the vision for what a just, peaceful, prosperous world can be before it comes into being. What kind of being do you want to be? What kind of human beings' attitudes and behaviors do we want to foster and leave for the future after we're gone? What if the vast majority of human beings on this planet treated others the way they would want to be treated themselves? Do we want to live in a world where we generally cheat each other as human beings- environmentally- in our business practice- in our advertising or social networks? People eventually will not be separated and accorded respect based on skin color, or gender, or sexual orientation- and this should be what all of us want- because it is what we would want for ourselves as fellow individuals. We need to become better beings by evolving ourselves while fostering respective attitudes and working at phasing out the dis-respective ones. It's time to get everyone on board. How much better would your world be if most of the people you encountered shared a sense of positive community with you- who had their unique perspective to share with you as opposed to a world where people raced and competed to be the most conformist cultural ideal robot? Together we should expect- and behave with- reciprocity. In a socially shrinking world the individual choices you make matter. Your choices affect others. Your job choice- your plastic consumption. In an Anthropocene epoch where mankind is impacting the physical environment at an increasing rate some want the "freedom" to pollute someone else's environment. Some want the "freedom" to not wear a mask in a public place during a pandemic and risk passing on a deadly virus to someone else's relatives. It is relatively easy to just maximize any advantages that you didn't earn in a genetic lottery and be selfish without consideration for other fellow individuals who didn't have your advantages. It may be more profitable for you to just dump your industrial waste into your neighbor's climate but you have to decide if that's living the life you want to live.

Our shared planet's improvement is- on the whole- all about human attitudes. Now Russian political unrest or Asian epidemics are your direct problem because of connectivity. We humans can evolve ourselves into better beings or into monsters- or worse- cultural robots. Please embrace the individual attitude of individual respect and reciprocity and use these as higher societal values that connect us all.

11. We can do better than Conservatism and Liberalism in making progress with society and measure ourselves and our structures principally by individual respect and reciprocity.

We need to recognize address and fix the problems that are with liberal and conservative thinking that stray away from individual respect and reciprocity. Conservatism and Liberalism have become static tribal dogmas which at times don't let the individuals stuck inside these boxes (or waves of thought) integrate with others in society and explore new ideas, perspectives and solutions to social problems.

Conservatism at its worst could have the individual who has been born on 2nd base economically and won the genetic lottery believe his good fortune either the product of rugged self-reliance or providence and not honestly empathize with the fellow individual across the tracks who found themselves in less socially fortunate circumstances.

Liberalism- at it's worst- could deny the validity of the individual except as a cultural component who is permanently disadvantaged to a permanent conservative in power establishment and foster a disdain for individual achievement as inherently selfish and unsocial.

Instead of permanent sides or tribes fighting in perpetuity we can share the attitude of seeing fellow individuals who are all capable of good attitudes and values all based fundamentally on individual respect and reciprocity.

SIX

Your Story
(And Everyone Else's)

In the beginning there was you - as far as your personal story is concerned. This is not a statement of selfishness or narcissism or western cultural bias but of social reality- and as it turns out- your broadest and most honest basis of community with all your fellow human beings. As human beings we are each born as a blank slate culturally, religiously, linguistically, tribally, and even economically. Think back to your earliest memory. There very well may have been a Big Bang or God or both to create the universe before you arrived on this planet, but you were not around to see it- you would have to consider this information derived from other human beings born before you- people who considered (or unquestioningly accepted) this from other people in turn. Before you were exposed to and learned about language, culture (an esoteric social group identity), religion, race, ethnicity, nationality, heritage, ancestry, community, or even gender you began as a unique point of perspective on this planetary island other people long ago labeled (in the language they were taught from others) "Earth". Every other human being began just as you did in this way- people such as John Adams, Cleopatra, Pontius Pilate, Abraham Lincoln, Nelson Mandela, Adolph Hitler, Thomas Jefferson, Anne Frank, Osama Bin Laden, your neighbors next door, your daughter, and your great grandmother.

No one is born here Christian, Muslim, Black, White, Israeli, Palestinian, Hutu, Tutsi, Latina, American, Indigenous, etc. from their own perspective. We are essentially given a social identity from others after birth as if to say, "Welcome to planet Earth- your ancestors and parents were Christians, spoke English, regarded themselves fundamentally African American, Irish American, or Latino American, and so should you- we have a pre-determined social identity waiting for you". No one is, by complete definition, fundamentally American, Christian, Muslim, Black, White, Latina Catholic, Jewish, Palestinian, Hutu, Tutsi, etc. You either adopted these overgeneralized labels or they were associated with you. This is not to say that these descriptions of yourself- be they labels, lenses, advantages or cages are not real, or a significant component of who you are- but they are not fundamentally who you are socially. You may say that one step into the social world around you tells you that you are all about being black, or white, or Latina, or Asian, female, etc. and that others who look like you can identify with your circumstance more than others who do not look as you do- but who you are is much more fundamentally about what you personally think and do than what group you (or others) feel you belong to. Fundamentally who you are among everyone else is the unique pre-racial, pre-ethnic, pre-gender, pre-religious belief, pre-national, pre-cultural and pre-lingual pinpoint of perspective and personal values that you view the world from- and all other human beings are fundamentally walking human perspectives with personal values just as you are. We each have no choice in this fundamental individual identity among all others- we did not earn or deserve or contrive it- but we exist as it exists, and this is our most common link to our fellow human beings.

We have an inherent obligation to honesty and social reality to not let the culture we each walk through define who we fundamentally are among all other people. The first step in making our shared island a better place requires individual people recognizing that they themselves and all others are worthy of individual respect- regardless of race, ethnicity, gender, religion, nationality or culture. Being honest concerning your fundamental social identity allows you to recognize that no other human being is of a fundamentally different group than you are- there are no different breed of humans that live over there on the other side of the world- or in that other neighborhood. We begin at birth perceiving and questioning from our unique exclusive perspective and we should remain perceiving and questioning our cultural environment throughout our lives rather than just accepting our cultural socialization as the unquestioned definition of ourselves.

Your perspective looks out through a window on our shared world. You are wearing lenses of language and culture and maybe religion etc. that others gave you and a skin of race, ethnicity, gender, etc. You are not fundamentally- by definition- at your core among others- a woman or a man, white or black skinned, born again Christian or devout Muslim, Hutu or Tutsi, Palestinian or Israeli, American or British. Among all others you are fundamentally *a unique individual*- just as they are (even though they may not have recognized this fact).

Where did you get your information about the culture or religion that you may learn to feel so much a part of? You were a valid unique blank state of consciousness before you learned about your identity or social classification in the eyes of others or yourself- your DNA was unique, your body was unique, your every movement and motion in your mother's womb was unique. You and I gradually became aware, as we grew into our respective lives, about our social affiliation according to family, race, ethnicity, gender, nationality, and surrounding (and apparent link to past) culture, and we learned if we were assigned a religious or spiritual affiliation or were free to choose, or not choose, one of our own- just as our fellow human beings learned these things.

After birth we found ourselves growing socially through a context of psychological socialization which helped us to live on our planet with others, communicate through language, and find some sense of love, community, safety, security, warmth and enjoyment among our fellow individual human beings. We each live in some sort of social context- we have learned to become group members- we wear masks of culture over our individual perspective- and our perception of culture does influence us- but we are still unique individuals. We can form personal values- independent of, but sometimes largely influenced by, our perception of our surrounding culture- based on our unique perspective in our shared world.

Economics

As humans we have priorities of survival to deal with: first we must escape the Tiger or whatever immediate threat is chasing us- we must find someone to help us if we are incapacitated beyond self-help due to injury or illness- we must find and secure water, shelter and food- we must take care of any dependents we have- and if we're lucky we can find access to a marketplace to interact with to produce for ourselves by exchanging something we individually have to offer others. Through the process of socialization and wearing a mask of social context we may not have been made consciously aware that we, as human beings, each have by choice (if we are lucky enough to not be enslaved or imprisoned) generally five means of survival. We are all, as individuals, by birthright thrust into the inescapable context of social economics, and we each learn- consciously or subconsciously- that we can either:

1. burden to produce that with which we need to survive on our own independently --- rely solely on ourselves.
2. depend on others to voluntarily burden to produce for us --- rely on charity.
3. depend on others to involuntarily burden to produce for us--- rely on stealing from others.
4. speculate or gamble on the rising or falling of the value of an asset.
5. burden to produce that which we can or choose to- and exchange this or the fruits of this production with others- who exchange with us that which we do not produce--- voluntary individual exchange.

Almost every human being has only these five options of survival on our planet. As far as the implications of these: human survival in the long run requires individual human beings producing, whether it is creating healthcare, endeavoring to forage for food, or building shelter. To produce all that we need to survive or value on our own individually and independently for a lifetime is unlikely and time consuming. Try constructing a cell phone much less a pencil by yourself. All of us need to benefit from a certain amount of charity from others- as when we are very old and unable to produce for ourselves (insurance doesn't cover the human caring we will need that cannot be bought with dollars) -or very young (most of us would view this towards children as parental obligation and not charity in the traditional sense- but it is still charity in the sense that a child needs external help from others to survive). Most of us enjoy helping out the ones we love, our friends and others- but charity can overburden producers without rewarding them for their production- and as the old adage says: "Give a child a fish and she eats for a day- teach a child to fish and she eats for a lifetime"- if we really want to help others, we should teach them to help themselves as much as possible.

Since we are all fundamentally individuals among each other in shared context- the practice of taking from individuals by force possibly can violate ourselves (if they take from us as well) or those we care about as well as others- and most human beings feel this to be generally unethical- even independently underneath reference to established social codes of ethics from our religions and philosophies.

Number four is a form of gambling and since the only tangible gain is profit (often blind profit) above everything else- this cold pursuit of profit in itself may disregard other important factors in our human lives such as our natural environment (clean air, clean oceans, wildlife and ecosystems), the wellbeing and even safety of workers in industry, and the loss of jobs and homes of people without power or leverage who are affected by the far away transactions of other people's speculations, profits or losses.

The fifth option, voluntary individual exchange- through which we recognize and accept our inherent and natural basic unequal perspectives, actions, and production among others as a potential benefit for ourselves and others, is a luxury that more people have had the opportunity to benefit from recently than at any previous time in humanity's social evolution- is the basis for the human sustaining marketplace and involves the attitude that, individually and culturally, no one else fundamentally really owes us anything except justice, and we only really have a right to demand what we ourselves personally produce or receive through voluntary exchange- which amounts to an acceptance rather than a cultural denial of our accountable individuality. In this common world we share we have a responsibility among others to hold ourselves fundamentally personally accountable for our actions and production.

Although it is in our self-interest to have an attitude of producing for oneself to the best of one's ability it is important to recognize that individuals do not begin economically on the same level. There's nothing wrong with a kid who is born into privilege into a wealthy family- even though he didn't earn this social advantage. What is wrong is if he grows to believe that he has generally pulled himself up by his bootstraps and automatically looks down upon other kids born into the challenges of an environment of poverty as inferior or lazy- and doesn't identify with these poverty kids as "his people". There is nothing wrong with a kid who is born into poverty- it's the poverty not the kid that is the problem. What is wrong is if he grows to believe that others born into wealth and privilege are automatically bad people who didn't earn what they have fairly without knowing their individual story- and doesn't identify with them as his fellow individual people worthy of individual rights like himself. Both the rich kid and the poor kid victimize themselves when they automatically overgeneralize other fellow human beings as parts of bad groups they don't like and won't positively engage with. Instead, the rich kid has an opportunity to question the logic that all those individual people each born a blank slate like myself are raised in that disadvantaged poor area generation after generation because they all make poor choices and are inherently kind of bad people? And all these people in my affluent neighborhood have generationally had advantages in wealth, education, healthcare, etc. because they are inherently good people? This makes zero sense.

What if one of the poor neighborhood kids was taken as an infant and raised with all the advantages of the wealthy family while wealthy kid was raised in poverty? Does the environment that the individual is raised in matter?

The role of Government is to secure justice and promote the general welfare of all individuals within a certain jurisdiction. When individuals are born into mental illness or generational poverty or find themselves trapped in systemic disadvantages in education, safety, housing, food, and healthcare it is the role of government to help.

Ourselves among others

We live in a social world of fundamentally individual people many of whom unfortunately define themselves as group members according to race, ethnicity, gender, religion, nationality or culture. People defining themselves socially as anything other than fundamentally self-accountable individuals is the fuel for the war, racism, prejudice, terrorism, and economic problems that we have today. If we want to reduce or eliminate these problems- we need to teach young people to respect themselves and others as fundamentally self-accountable individuals socially.

None of us are fundamentally- at our core- static nouns like "white Anglo-Saxon protestants", "Latinas", "black or white people". Socially we are much more fundamentally verb-like fellow evolving individuals if we are to be honest with ourselves.

We each begin as valid, individual unique points of perspective- and our unique perspective and point of action (our personal accountability among all others) never goes away throughout our lives here. We must deal with the context of a human body with human desires and satisfactions, emotions and limitations. All human beings share this beginning and ongoing reality in common. Our common individuality in social context is our most fundamental and inclusive bridge of community with all other people- and it is the basis for why individual rights should be so highly regarded worldwide across perceived borders of race, ethnicity, gender, religion, nationality and culture. All human beings share an individual validity in social context together.

Getting along together

It is easier for individual people to identify with and get along with each other than nations, cultures or religions to get along. When people suddenly find themselves in an elevator or subway with others of perceived diverse racial, ethnic, gender, religious, national or cultural groups- they tend to instinctively behave according to a prioritization of individual respect- and put cultural expectations temporarily in the background. Individual respect instinctively comes first socially- cultural respect (which we learn from the limited and happenstance experiences in the social environment we have found ourselves in- and that others may not have experienced) should always come afterward.

To live among others is to restrict your personal freedom and cultural expectations somewhat- we each must defer to basic individual respect.

Alone we can define ourselves however we want to- but the instant we share the company of others we become fundamentally, first and foremost, self-accountable individuals among each other. Because we are each and all individuals- individual respect is commonly beneficial generally and individual rights make sense among everybody. Cultural values and expectations may be shared among certain groups but not all individuals. When cultural values (which may be relevant only to some) conflict with individual respect (which is always relevant to all) - individual respect must be prioritized if we are to live in a just society.

The social conflicts we have as human beings (war, prejudice, racism, terrorism, ethnic oppression, sexism, economic stagnation) are generally fueled by people defining themselves (and others) in their own minds first and foremost as separate cultural group members rather than fundamentally fellow members of a whole community of individuals worthy of individual respect. We do not fundamentally live in a world of Muslims, Christians, Jews, Americans, French, Latinas, Men or Women, working class, Bourgeoisie, etc.- this overgeneralization of ourselves into fixed permanent categories fosters social disharmony because it discourages people from being honest about recognizing others as basically fellow human beings, underneath and across race, ethnicity, gender, religion, nationality and culture. Those "other people" across the world are your people on a fundamental social level before levels of learned language, culture or religion. If our world is to become a better place socially- young people internationally need to be introduced to the reality that culture (esoteric social groups that individual human beings learn to socialize in to) has never and will never make anyone intrinsically who they are.

Culture

It would be terrible to lose the richness, beauty and lessons that 100's or 1000's of years of distinct cultural ideals bring to our contemporary existence. Culture provides life paths, ideals, schools of thought and lenses through which our individual perspectives can journey. Culture can be a wonderful thing- and it may be necessary for a person's wellbeing- but culture should serve people- not the other way around- and should not separate human beings from interacting with each other positively individually. If our culture directs us to act disrespectfully, inhumanely, or eat unhealthily- we should tell our culture no. We each exist and have personal validity and personal values outside the context of culture- which can separate human beings. Cultural groups sweep up individual people like you and I and those we go to war against.

We become slaves to culture in a bad way when we forget or disregard a basic individual respect for ourselves and all others and instead define ourselves in totality or near totality by a culture that we are individually journeying through. Many people live their lives on cultural autopilot. To define ourselves and other people fundamentally by broad generalizations of race, ethnicity, gender, religion, nationality, or culture is a too seldom recognized act of prejudice- and in many cases an act of dishonesty with oneself and others. Deep down we know better than to limit the definition of whom we and others are- and can be.

Are you spending more of your life attempting to carefully conform to cultural ideals or exploring the full potential of who you (and others) individually can be within and beyond cultural parameters? You have lost yourself if your clothes, car, colloquialisms, entertainment choices, opinions, etc. are principally for conforming to culture. You're not living your own life but simply roleplaying to a perception of perceived cultural expectations. It is fine and normal to participate in culture but not to lose your personal identity and self-direction in the process. If young people are raised so that if they were removed from their familiar culture they could adapt to being transported to another social context without their previous culture's values - then we are headed for a better world. If a young person would completely fall apart as an individual if removed from their culture and could never adapt and cope to a new cultural context- that young person is much too entrenched in their culture to help bridge a broader sense of community in our shared world.

People are primarily unique individual evolving points of perspective with a collection of experiences, personality, and learned values who learn from, befriend, love, disagree with, and hopefully respect others and are worthy of some measure of individual respect themselves. If this talk of the individual sounds selfish or lonely it is not- after all a prerequisite to loving someone else is a separate distinct being- apart from oneself. A cosmos all to oneself- as one being (or pretending to be one being) without the distinction of any others- would be a very lonely place indeed. We need an "other" to not be lonely. Our greatest and broadest sense of community comes from respecting ourselves individually and recognizing others as fellow individual people that we share life with and who are worthy of individual respect just as we are.

How do we know what we think we know?

Because you begin in this world an individual- where does your knowledge about everything else come from? How did you learn about God or Islam or Christianity, Judaism, or Atheism? If you are to be honest with yourself and with your religion- religion must always begin with you and not with "we" or "God".

You and I and everyone else were born before we learned about culture or religion or affiliations with others. Honestly you must always begin with yourself receiving information. We learn about Religion and culture from other people while ideals such as goodness or vileness we seem to have an experience of inherently. We are all in touch with our ideals through our conscience. We may find ideals that we are willing to subordinate ourselves to- or even live for- such as goodness. Certain ideals we may even value so much that we place them before our individual physical being.

We must be careful because religion and culture at times can lead individuals away from personal accountability and individual empathy (putting ourselves in the shoes of other fellow individuals who are in a different social context). If there is ever a conflict between religion or culture and individual rights- we must always prioritize individual rights. We must never allow religion or culture to prevent us from respecting or empathizing with the individual in all living things.

What do you want?

What does "self-interest" really mean? How would you want to have lived your life? Being kind or helpful for example or materialistic or hurting your planet? As an individual do you want to live in a world where you only feel community with a relatively small esoteric fixed tribe of people or would you rather have a greater sense of community with everyone? Should we embrace values that make us feel good about ourselves and others such as being there for family member support or Love or treating our planet well? We ought to be honest with ourselves- even if only for our own self-respect and a basic respect for other fellow human beings. We each have limited time and limited lives and must choose how to spend that time on our own unique life path. As an individual you would most certainly like to feel good about yourself and have as clean a conscience as possible. Is how you live your life important to you? Would you want to have lived just for money? Is making an effort at producing for yourself and your family a priority? Can you "pay yourself" in conscience and principle and peace of mind as to doing the right thing- not stepping out of your conscience to make a sale or overlook the environment for profit, etc.?

It can be tough to try to relax and enjoy a mountain retreat with a guilty conscience. What kind of world do you want your children to grow into? Would you rather see a generally peaceful and pleasant world around you than an unpeaceful unpleasant one- a world of peaceful community more than one of pain and conflict? Is a world where others are happy and educated or impoverished and disenfranchised a good environment for you to live in? Would you rather share a world with others who have access to education, healthcare and meaningful employment or with others who don't have these things? At the end of your life are you going to be proudest of how honest and kind and hard-working you were, how you lived - or of how much you own?

If you would not like to be limited or disadvantaged because of the color of your skin does it make sense to you that others would not either? Would you like to generally be free to produce for yourself? Shouldn't others have this opportunity as well? Do you want to be respected for what you do without advantages on your merit and like to see others judged on their merit? Do you want to like or dislike someone automatically because of skin color or nationality or religion? Do you want to be regarded principally as the unique individual that you actually are in society and among all other people?

You have skin in the game in the shared world you inhabit with others. If adopting certain attitudes would contribute to making our shared world a significantly better place for you and others, would you do it? Human Capital benefits you and all other humans and our Earth. The attitudes and behavior of others affects you now in a socially shrinking world. You have the power to initiate peace from your space and perspective by being the change you want to see in our world.

SEVEN

//

Our Story- Individual
means Community

We each live on a common planetary island- and our planet is shrinking socially- our neighbors are moving closer to us as we are to them- so for the sake of peace and prosperity among ourselves as individual people (our most common denominator) we need to consider constructing some common, more unifying social bridges among each other- together- a common language underneath race, ethnicity, gender, religion, nationality or culture. This language should be based on the pre-cultural primary individual identities in social context that we each and all share and can relate to personally- it is called the language of individual respect.

How many of us actively cultivate a strong sense of individual value for ourselves or others? Every day we are defined and over-generalized as fundamentally Americans, Latinas, feminists, African Americans, White Americans, poor or rich, Muslims or Christians, Conservatives or Liberals, or some other social classification- so much so that it can be an uphill battle expressing oneself, or recognizing the value of others, individually in society.

Individuality is prerequisite to personal and social accountability. You and I, regardless of our race, ethnicity, gender, religion, nationality or culture, whether we were raised of wealthy means in Massachusetts or poor in Chiapas, devout in Pakistan, or oppressed in Ireland, whether we classify ourselves as Buddhists, Christians, Muslims, Jews, Communists, Feminists, Capitalists, Hispanics, or Baptists, are fundamentally self-accountable individual human beings living among each other in the context of this planet we each live on- and so is/was everyone else who has ever lived here or who will ever live here. We are "self-accountable" because 1. we each are made up of a unique physical identity in ourselves- which is not exactly like any other- ever- 2. we each have a sense of unique perspective- 3. we live among other individuals of other unique perspectives in the same global village- 4. we enact actions from ourselves which affect others. As a result of these conditions, we inherit an automatic lateral accountability among our fellow human beings regardless of the racial, ethnic, gender, religious, national, or cultural social contexts we have each found ourselves in the midst of. We are personally accountable regardless of ours or other's judgment about ourselves. We each exist in a fundamental sense as valid, independent, individual human beings- and our perspectives and actions stem from ourselves and no one else- not our culture, not our ancestors, not our communities nor our temples, churches, mosques, or peer groups (we may believe that they originate from God or some other source- but they stem from us or at least through ourselves among others)- none of our current established world religions dispute this in their referential doctrine- they do not deny the accountability of the individual among others at a basic level. Our personal accountability is not a moral choice- it is a shared basic biological reality we each have found ourselves having to deal with among others.

We, each and all, have found ourselves here having to deal with the context of our planet on our own unique path- and we have this in common with every human being who has ever lived, is living, or ever will live. You and I are linked to all others through this shared predicament of individual uniqueness in a shared context. We are each inherently and naturally unequal among each other. No one has ever or will ever dream the exact same dreams, inhabit the exact same physical body, think the exact same thoughts, see, imagine, move, act or love from the exact same perspective- through the exact same moment. You and I are special- evolving personally, constantly and momentarily- never quite the same person from second to second- but our personal evolution is distinct from any other's evolution- and if we weren't separate, different and distinct from one another, we wouldn't have anyone to love or share with. The concept of the individual is not an ethnocentric value of Western contemporary civilization- you and

I and everyone else are intrinsically unique in the universe- and each and every human being always has been and always will be.

All human beings also share another common beginning- we - among our various races, ethnicities, genders, religions, nationalities and cultures- are all literally members of the same biological family descended from common human ancestors. At least 30,000 years ago, these distant relatives of ours roamed as individuals cooperating in the context of small groups, lifetime after lifetime for thousands of years, across parts of our planet existing as scavengers, gatherers, hunters, or raiders of other groups. Individuals probably encountered individuals of other groups only either through warring against them or exchanging with them. Each person in these groups had to deal with the five means of survival just as you and I do. The exact social structure of each particular group was unknown without surviving record but individual freedom of self- expression for most was likely socially overshadowed by cooperation in the persistent unsafe daily struggle for immediate survival- as is, of course, unfortunately the same circumstance for many people today. Many of these distant relatives of ours eventually developed speech and language which allowed them to share ideas and construct a common culture of belief of how to deal with their surrounding context which could be passed on to children and generations- just as your family or local culture did with you. These people likely felt some sense of community within their cultural tribe and had a human somewhat positive psychologically socialized notion of social familiarity within their group and a somewhat negative perception of unfamiliarity of groups outside their own- much like many of their distant family members- us. Many no doubt, like ourselves, found some comfort in their perception of the specific historical traditions and belief systems which had been passed down through generations among their perceived group and family members. Many of these traditions and innovations were pragmatic instructions as to what had worked and not worked in the past through trial and error in the experience of other past individuals- other traditions were an attempt by group leaders to reinforce the structure of the group. If they were like many cultural groups of their time and today- they placed special comfort and emotional reverence particularly for individuals and events that, they were told, existed and took place long, long ago and far, far away from their personal experience of the present- perhaps the alleged origins of their tribe's cultures, religions, and traditions. Whether or not the "long ago" individuals and events were in fact more "important" than the present day audience of individuals and their present day experience and circumstances is, at least, a matter of perspective- but it is clear that the cultural tribal storytellers played a significant role in emotionally and intellectually persuading many of these present day individuals that they were inherently a relatively small part of a larger, more significant cultural whole rooted relatively deep before the existence of the individual audience member- and this "cultural whole" reinforced their feelings of the fundamental separation of themselves from other perceived cultural groups- leading many of the audience members to begin to define themselves socially as tribal or cultural group members.

You may remember being taught in school that around 10,000 to 7000 years ago some of these group members began to shift from hunting and gathering to farming and domesticating animals. This shift was no doubt due in at least some part to certain individuals in the previous groups escaping routine survival skills and rote cultural role playing long enough to think creatively in new directions apart from the crowd leading to new ideas and discoveries for their group (or other exchanging or conquering groups)- thus influencing other individuals in the group into new ways of thinking about how to manage themselves. The stability of sources of food from farming and domestication involved the settlement of these agrarian groups and their relative prosperity attracted other tribal groups who were assimilated- creating larger settlements- which developed into socially complex societies. Specialized trades and common currency eventually developed as support structures and as populations grew and condensed mass hierarchical power structures developed to maintain order and stability. Religious leaders and autocrats often took power- some individuals who came to be regarded as closer to- or more in touch with- perceived deities, the forces of nature and fate than other individuals- and many group leaders- often using emotional appeal to the crowd- gained the power of quantitative force through their followers over others in the community. Group members are easier for autocrats to manipulate in mass than individuals. All these group members within their families, communities, tribes, religious and governing structures were still fundamentally self-accountable individuals- men, women, slaves, priests and autocrats- still dealing individually with the four means of survival- but these "societal" individuals had to deal with defining themselves in society among subcultures of cultures- they were dominated by complex cultural restriction- perhaps putting the extent of their personal accountability and even validity into question among themselves (not unlike the possible confusion over personal accountability and validity in our complex contemporary global society). They learned to wear masks of cultures within culture- playing social roles expected of them within society- and many, no doubt, like many today, found refuge and even comfort from personal accountability and responsibility in attempting to define their own individual journey of life through wearing these external masks. One of these masks was the common language that they shared among each other- whereas language is inherently a restricted set of symbols that describe the world- and no language contains symbols for everything that may be described- this allowed them to conform to and share a more common perspective among those who used it as their means of communication- alienating somewhat others of other perceived groups who did not communicate through that general interpretation of the world. Another mask was the sense among individuals that they could take credit generally for the achievements of other individuals within their group- such as: long, long ago so and so was reported to achieve that great achievement- and so and so was a member of our perceived group- therefore "we" are proudly associated with the achievements of so and so.

Eventually in some of the world's developing tribes, communities, and societies increased literacy and writing evolved through the gradual self-expression of, and for, those apart from the elite allowing for more and more exchange of ideas among all individuals- while increased community stabilization eventually left more time and, in some cases, slightly more freedom and tolerance of individual expression- for people expressing their exclusively unique personal perspectives. People needed to think in new directions apart from the crowd to create invention, successful businesses, art, and discover scientific advances. Through a small minority of these societies (and other tribal cultures left apart from the aggregate) a gradual, perhaps subliminal, progressive climb was made through individual to individual from an environment where they were taught to define themselves as inherently part of the collective and thought themselves fundamentally subjugated to their culture, following a rote pattern of social role playing, based on emulating social ideals which did not concretely exist in reality (as no one is a perfect example of an ideal), for the major social purpose of supporting the powerful that were in place above them- onto one where individual by individual began to emerge from the crowd defying cultural definition of themselves and gradually creating more freedom opportunity and advancement for others, contributing to a better life for those others in community/society, even society leaders. People began to define themselves and not simply accept their perceived surrounding culture's definition of them- defining their own values through making personal decisions instead of automatically following rote patterns of cultural cues. The small minority of humankind's eventual establishment of "Democracy"- at first one man-one vote eventually evolving into one individual-one vote showed some sign of promise for individual freedom but was also, as it is now as well, an institution that usually established group power over individual power- and remains a weapon for some principally to forcibly redistribute what does not belong to them from other's production. If nine out of ten people vote to steal from the tenth person- the latter was a victim of Democracy. Democracy recognizes quantitative accountability- one's vote as a number- and allocates power of quantitative force among voters in common over others- encouraging group cohesion- but true individual freedom in society demands that qualitative accountability to be recognized- one's expression and elaboration of one's unique perspective and the fundamental recognition and respect of the sub-cultural honest expression of the unique perspectives of others.

In the so called "developed" and "developing" world- the contemporary civilization which resulted from the socially suppressed but enduring individually celebratory aspirations of people which were based on- and fueled by- evolving more and more freedom and expression for individual people- without respect as a rule, to caste, race, ethnicity, gender, religion, nationality, or culture- through voluntary individual exchange- is called the marketplace. This has evolved from exchanging among individuals in the first human gatherings and settlements to be the most productive way contemporary human beings sustain ourselves as a species- despite social pressure to define ourselves as merely a part of culture- but rather finding a grounding in what we can personally build, innovate and relate to, and cooperate with others self determinately as individual people- breaking away at least somewhat from merely imitating social ideals as objects of the social structure.

The marketplace is based on the fifth option human beings have for survival- that is- one of us decides to produce something of perceived value to others- using mind, body or both- and voluntarily exchanges this with someone else and receives something of perceived value in return- as opposed to generally attempting to forcibly redistribute the production of other individuals through central or quantitative force of power. This is the basic philosophy that Israeli Americans and Palestinian Americans, or Tutsi Americans and Hutu Americans, or Serbian Americans and Croatian Americans may have when they exchange among each other in America, for example- they decide to exchange individually underneath and across their cultural affiliations. Participants in the global marketplace who have the opportunity to exchange with others what they have to offer in order to receive what they cannot exchange for in their local culture- live in the most productive societies in terms of economic productivity and opportunity of self-determination among their fellow citizens (even the poor of which are generally better off than the poor of our other societies) -but this opportunity has not yet reached all of us in the contemporary human family.

The marketplace is made up of, and fueled by, individual exchange- but is currently often filtered through entities called corporations- which, by definition, are government-chartered businesses made exempt by the former from certain areas of accountability towards other businesses or individuals. Many of these are large, hierarchically structured, and bureaucratic and, although they survive directly by the individual exchange of ideas and production of their associates and customers (which result from allowing individual freedom from central and quantitative social power to create and innovate) their size and structure often subjugate individual accountability and innovation to team role playing and cooperation in the name of efficiency. At worst, their freedom from accountability can lead to abuses of power of group leaders- and bureaucratic structure can lead to an overly hierarchical, almost dictatorial, restriction of individual freedom and innovation of producers within the business. They can be indifferent to environmental degradation and culturally insensitive- but if positive personal potential can evolve through community and society, it can evolve through corporations, and their size and scope can benefit individuals by reaching those who would not otherwise have an opportunity to participate in offering their exchange in production with the global marketplace- and this marketplace is their means to market power to achieve what they value- including environmental and cultural protection. The marketplace, at its core, is simply a tool for rewarding people with what they perceive they value- it is much more powerful for achieving this than governmental power or even cultural power over the long run- because markets adapt to change quicker than cultures do- and respond to individuals- while governments and cultures redistribute power and influence among esoteric groups of people. Markets generally reward production without caring about the race, ethnicity, gender, religion, nationality, or culture of the producer -unfortunately some powerful cultural group members who participate in markets do care- but the marketplace in practice rewards production over prejudice. Markets, as human functionaries, blindly respect what individuals produce and value- and markets have played, and can play, a virtuous role in individual freedom from negative cultural restriction and in the development of evolutionary prosperity and sustainability for people- and what people care about- they offer opportunities to individuals. But the marketplace owes no one anything- it has never "failed" anyone- it's not "supposed" to "take care of" anybody- it embodies no accountability in itself- only the humans who interact with it are accountable.

The United States of America is currently the most economically productive, powerful nation on earth because it is the world's most powerful market economy- it has the most powerful market economy because it is historically the place where more of the human family has left the perceived negative cultural restrictions of their previous cultures and concentrated and mixed to exchange personal production with the least individually restrictive values of culture according to race, ethnicity, gender, religion, nationality or local culture in the world. It is the largest human gathering place where individuals and individual achievement are generally celebrated more than group affiliation and group achievement (just barely- but generally).

Groups don't make decisions, don't love and don't care, individuals do- sharing their unique perspectives with each other. We need to find ways to become a world more-so of free interacting individuals and less-so of restricted group members if we are to empower ourselves to make the world a better place for ourselves and others. We need to remember and teach our children that Governments and corporations can be co-opted by group control- and concentrate power- but markets fundamentally serve individual values in the long run- they diversify power- (there are many more wealthy citizens- and much more diversity among who is wealthy and who is powerful over their own lives- in market countries than non-market ones). Markets are a cross cultural means of achieving this diversification of power underneath and across race, ethnicity, gender, religion, nationality, or culture.

People voluntarily offer their individual production by enlisting as producers in the marketplace- on terms mutually agreeable to themselves and the exchanging party- because they feel it is a better opportunity than any other alternative they have individually at the time- from a man applying to work as an assembly worker in a US/Mexico border town maquiladoras- to a woman applying for a management position with Microsoft- this is the same case. If you are of the bent to criticize the market as not allocating resources to your liking- try living in an anti-market dictatorship- or living on your own in a forest- chances are that you participate in a marketplace voluntarily yourself- and the freedom, self-determination and expression through which you have expressed your opinion- along with your ability to help others- have, in no small part, been provided by the marketplace. More funds for addressing poverty and healthcare in the "third" world- along with those that fund world environmental efforts- come from the United states and other market countries, by far, than any other source in the world. Government- which is absolutely necessary in society to promote the general welfare where the profit motive does not or falls short- is funded by the marketplace. Even anti-market protest forces are funded by the marketplace. The marketplace is the most widespread source of human sustainability in the history of mankind. By definition- market entities do not force anyone to work for them against their will- offering only perceived opportunities on mutually agreed terms between exchangers.

People are inherently self-accountable among others, we must deal with the five means of survival, and the marketplace is a place where we may find an outlet from the perceived negative restrictions of the social environment's we have found ourselves raised in the midst of such as caste, race, ethnicity, gender, religion, nationality and culture- and yet we can still maintain what we feel is important from our culture into our personal identity. We don't have to necessarily live individualistically to remember that we are fundamentally self-accountable among each other- we just must remember the advantages holding ourselves and others accountable- and the historical and logical consequences of not recognizing the fundamental accountability of ourselves and others. We should not lose ourselves in any culture- whether it's ethnic, conservative, liberal or corporate culture- so we need to celebrate our personal values underneath cultural values. We need to work to build an inclusive environment which places individual respect above restrictive social culture and build a larger sense of community among ourselves. We need to foster attitudes of personal accountability and three individually responsive social structures to govern ourselves together: Marketplaces to sustain and empower ourselves for our own and each other's improvement, while diversifying power in society- democracy to maintain rule of law, provide education, health insurance and empower government to act in those cases where the profit motive doesn't promote the general welfare- and constitutional protections of individual rights to umpire democracy.

EIGHT

///

From the Right

A white skinned individual who identifies herself as an American Conservative may say that she prioritizes individual liberty and freedom in America as a core value and may also value the sanctity of life and the Christian faith as well. One of her fellow Americans devoted his entire life to individual liberty and freedom for Americans- he was successful- and was deliberately killed for his efforts- he also was a devout Christian minister who was willing to sacrifice his life for the liberty and freedom of his fellow Americans- he just happened to be an American who had black skin instead of white- his name was Martin Luther King Jr. On January 12th, 1987 conservatives in the state of Arizona rescinded an executive order causing Arizona to become the only state to de-recognize Martin Luther King Jr. Day. When some individuals who identify themselves as conservatives speak of individual liberty and freedom and Christian principles they evidently are not including, in their mind's eye, those fellow individual Americans who suffered under black codes and Jim Crow laws. Do these white skinned conservatives identify and empathize with a fellow American individual who is perceived as a threat or potential criminal simply because he has black skin? Where is the opportunity for individual freedom and liberty for that fellow individual? How easy is it for that person to define themselves as a "free individual" while they are constantly being profiled, stereotyped, and defined by others by the color of their skin?

Many people who dislike "liberals" (or "conservatives") are confused about who *their people* are- *they* are potentially *your people* simply with different attitudes. Human beings have the capacity to develop attitudes that will make our country better for all of us and the rest of our world. In the near future America can be a place where all persons are fundamentally judged and respected individually- a country where almost everyone identifies with everyone else as a fellow individual first and a group member according to skin color, ethnicity, gender, sexual orientation, physical challenge such as deafness or blindness, or religion, or culture, or political party only afterward. Together we can build a nation where prosperity is generally created through the individual exchange of production, work ethic, and cooperation with our fellow individuals throughout our shared world fostered by a belief that no one should be hampered by systemic discrimination and the understanding that government is a tool for justice and the production of human needs in areas where the profit motive private sector falls short of those needs.

We individuals often throw ourselves into- and can sometime lose ourselves in- waves of already established thought, religion or culture. American Conservatism is one such wave. Our American national creed- "All men are created equal"- means that all people in our country should be recognized, regarded and generally treated as equal citizens. Racism and sexism as well as other forms of discrimination against groups in America has systemically targeted our fellow Americans and it is our patriotic duty to treat all citizens equally. An America founded and based on individual freedom where segments of the population have been systematically oppressed because of their skin color or gender has never yet achieved greatness.

History

A Wikipedia article on the topic of American conservatism has mentioned the following attitudes and values that have been associated with conservative belief- "tax cuts, a greatly increased US military budget, deregulation, appeals to family values and conservative Christian morality. Conservative voters typically oppose abortion, gun control, and gay marriage. Other modern conservative beliefs include opposition to a world government (a view shared with many anti-globalists on the political left), skepticism about the importance or validity of certain environmental issues, the importance of self-reliance instead of reliance on the government to solve problems, support for the state of Israel, support for prayer in the public schools, opposition to gun control, opposition to embryonic stem cell research, support for a strong Law and Order policy, strict enforcement of the law, and long jail terms for repeat offenders".

Of course, not all people who call themselves conservative have all of these attitudes and values. There are those who call themselves pro-choice conservatives or atheist conservatives, social conservatives or fiscal conservatives, and those who simply may define themselves under the umbrella term of conservative because they want a sense of community with what their parents- or perceived culture- believes or believed in the past etc. Some other attitudes among some who consider themselves conservatives may or may not include:

- the belief that nature should be primarily subordinate, conquered and controlled by man as opposed to the idea that man is a part of nature and specifically an animal part of nature and related biologically to all other life on our planet.
- a willingness to follow a religious text such as the Bible as an ultimate backstop reality that should not be questioned or that God as the believed author should not be questioned.
- a strong desire and attempt to preserve a cultural time and place and value system as in a nostalgic "good old days" that may have not been quite as good as their memory and quite often not good for fellow individuals of different minority skin color or gender groups.

Conservativism and Individual Respect

On the bright side of Conservatism, the concept of the individual is acknowledged, at least in theory, as important socially although often subjugated to culture and particularly religion. Conservatives generally respect the idea of individual exchange in the marketplace understanding that much of what human's need must be produced by other humans and exchanging individual production is more just and effective than general forced redistribution of that which you did not produce from someone else.

On the dark side of Conservatism, the word individual is often associated with an individualism that does not take into account the context of one individual's social advantages due to skin color or gender etc. which end up propping up certain esoteric groups of individuals rather than individuals as a whole. White conservatives have used the terms individual, individual initiative, and self-reliance towards black and brown skinned people, overlooking the reality that these people their entire lives have not been treated as equal individuals and therefore their social reality has forced them to deal with and regard their skin color as a dominant element of their social identity. Some American Conservatives have appropriated the term individual rights for mainly white male persons while it is harder for a minority person to be respected as an individual. It is hard to regard yourself as a free individual when it feels as if the whole world is conspiring to treat you as a skin color or a perception of how a woman should behave. The term individual was convenient to demand the respect of individual rights and private property protection that in many cases were enjoyed not just by individual initiative but as a result of a year by year built up system of the social advantage for one particular group of individuals- Red Lining in Chicago- Jim Crow laws in the south.

One of America's pre-eminent social problems is the attitude among some that America should be for and about white skinned people. Every white skinned American conservative should ask themselves- if their college daughter came home one day and announced that she was dating a black young man- how would they feel about it? If they were upset by that notion- towards a stranger that they know nothing of other than skin color- then they simply have a racial prejudice problem- it is as simple as that- and that is a challenge that they should work on if they want to live their life consistent with individual respect and American values. Lurking in places under the umbrella of conservatism are also some attitudes that go against the founding premise of America that "all men are created equal" such as a favorability for white skinned traditional Christian individuals to be in power over others or for female individuals to be paid less than their male counterparts for the same work achievement (see Gentleman's Agreement- The Equal Rights Amendment). The lack of individual empathy attitude that American individuals are inherently better or superior or more entitled than those individuals "unfortunate" enough to have been born in Syria or Zimbabwe, Honduras, Iran or wherever else- as if those born here had somehow inherently earned or deserved their birthright and socioeconomic head start above individuals born elsewhere- shows no respect for the "all men are created equal" foundation of our nation.

One of the biggest conservative myths is that the belief that the vast majority of American individuals who consistently struggle financially are doing so because of their own misbehavior- while in reality most poor American individuals are born into long established social environments of blight where there is little economic opportunity, education to get to opportunity, and plenty of initial and consistent systemic discrimination against them.

There is also the attitude that "as long as I'm ok and making money and comfortable I don't care about other individual's individual rights or opportunities and I don't need to reflect on where I began socially compared to others". Our fellow Americans who happen to have black skin were not experiencing life, liberty, and the pursuit of happiness in Selma, Alabama in 1964. As Americans these are our people and have always been our people- *your* fellow individual persons who are *your fellow Americans*. Were they caught in contexts where they were more likely to be lynched, jailed or shot- where you might not have been caught in that social circumstance as a white individual? Did they have equal access to health care or good jobs in proportion to those of another skin color?

Empathy

> *"We ought to consider what is the end of government, before we determine which is the best form. Upon this point all speculative politicians will agree, that the happiness of society is the end of government, as all Divines and moral Philosophers will agree that the happiness of the individual is the end of man. From this principle it will follow, that the form of government which communicates ease, comfort, security, or, in one word, happiness, to the greatest number of persons, and in the greatest degree, is the best." - John Adams*

What is best for all individuals, each of us, generally? First- in the name of personal accountability- it may be helpful to ask honestly how did I or others begin in the world of fellow individuals around us? What was my early life or formative social environment and circumstances compared to others? As an American individual you could have been born and raised in Pakistan or Libya and it is purely chance that you call yourself American and not Libyan or Pakistani. You certainly didn't build or earn your birthright of social advantage here. What unearned systemic social opportunities or conditions, advantages or disadvantages have you had compared to other individuals because of your skin color, social class connections, gender, or religion?

Are you identifying with all of your fellow human beings first and foremost as fellow individuals like yourself? Can you identify who a real American is by what skin color they have or what music they listen to or movies they watch or what religion they are or what dialect or colloquialisms they have? Have you pulled yourself up by your bootstraps for your success in life without the help of your family background, access to education, network opportunities, access to healthcare, etc. that was provided to you in the environment that you grew up in? Do large numbers of Americans grow up in environments where they are judged and immediately discriminated against because of the color of their skin or gender or sexual orientation? Do these people have a systematic disadvantage in society compared to other more socially fortunate individuals? Is it much, much, more difficult for these individuals to achieve success in society than those born under more fortunate circumstances- or are they disadvantaged because they just inherently have unsuccessful attitudes? On the whole are people poor because they would rather not work and make lazy decisions while financially "successful" people are well off because they generally have been virtuous? Is the USA doing ok if most citizens are not doing well but you're doing fine?

Reciprocity

We were founded on the conviction and premise that "all men are created equal" and if this attitude is not pervasive in our country, we won't live up our national creed- which is based on individual respect. Great things have happened in America for groups of individuals, but America will never be truly great until it lives up to its founding ideal that all men are created equal and its logical conclusions that all should be respected individually and that all generally have opportunity regardless of their skin color or gender or sexual orientation or physical ability or religious or non-religious affiliation etc.

Government

The role of government is to promote the general welfare among individuals in the aggregate in areas where the private for-profit marketplace either falls short or is indifferent to human needs.

Adam Smith, John Locke and George Orwell were all fans of government and the role of government to help the disadvantaged. In Smith's Wealth of Nations Book 5, Chapter One, Part three he argues *"The third and last duty of the sovereign or commonwealth is that of erecting and maintaining those public institutions and those public works, which, though they may be in the highest degree advantageous to a great society, are, however, of such a nature that the profit could never repay the expense to any individual or small number of individuals, and which it therefore cannot be expected that any individual or small number of individuals should erect or maintain. The performance of this duty requires, too, very different degrees of expense in the different periods of society.*

After the public institutions and public works necessary for the defence of the society, and for the administration of justice, both of which have already been mentioned, the other works and institutions of this kind are chiefly those for facilitating the commerce of the society, and those for promoting the instruction of the people. The institutions for instruction are of two kinds: those for the education of youth, and those for the instruction of people of all ages."

Capitalism needs government- businesses need boundaries of law. Smith's invisible hand of the marketplace illuminates the for-profit system as mankind's greatest tool for human development on this planet- but this system does not produce well in areas where there is no profit incentive for the private sector or in areas where the profit motive should be curtailed. It would be profitable for some businesses to hire poor children as laborers rather than have them go to school- so we needed government to enact child labor laws. It is politically better for us as citizens to have a national military that is accountable to all of us (in theory) than a private sector one which is loyal to only a few of us. It may not be profitable for the private sector to distribute vaccines or internet communication access or even electricity to rural areas and so we may use government for that purpose. In the case of health insurance if it is a biological fact of life that human beings get sick or injured and if the citizenry out of humane and economic reasons desires that all citizens have affordable comprehensive health insurance and the profit motive doesn't incentivize private insurance businesses to sustain universal comprehensive coverage- this is an area (like funding our military) where government will be needed to provide the coverage funded by taxation of the citizenry in the most fair form possible. This government service does not need to be socialism- it could be funded in part by a national sales tax that all persons who purchase US goods or services pay a small percentage towards. Anyone who buys a product or service- a stick of gum or an internet service- whether they be and undocumented immigrant or a foreign tourist- would pay into the system that they might need to use. Additional benefit from this system would be gained from unburdening employers from the cost and liability of providing coverage along with the advantage to workers, employees, contractors, or small business start-ups from worrying about access for themselves or their families- regardless of if they switched jobs or not- perhaps stimulating entrepreneurship.

Unfortunately, since we humans are morally imperfect, we need government to protect not only life and private property but to guard against damaging or destroying the natural terrarium that we live in- to safeguard against the swindle of precious resources and pollution of the environment of the less educated- and to enforce fair taxation. 95% of our American Redwood forest was felled for profit. We found it necessary to enact child labor laws to protect children from businessmen. American war profiteers were supplying Nazi Germany with munitions in the build-up of the Third Reich. Short term profiteering above wise stewardship has led us to man caused climate repercussions on a planetary scale. Few attitudes are more foolish than that of a stupid little man who decides to destroy, poison, or desecrate the terrarium that he was born into, that he is a biological part of, that he lives in, in order that he may profit in the short term but damage his (and others) environment for generations or forever. Lacking any sense of honor or virtue- this thief steals his spoils from future generations and the environment that nurtured him. Let us hope that this little man grows up. Oil that was once viewed as buried treasure has now been illuminated as buried potential poison.

There may come a time in your life after you have met Maslow's primaries- escaped from the tiger chasing you- attained water, food, shelter- etc. when you may have the luxury of deciding how you are going to live your life. Then faced with the 5 means of survival you must decide if you are going to gain money from exploiting the environment or others around you or are you going to have a moral compass for your own sake and place limits on what you are willing to do to make money. Unfortunately, every day around our world too many fathers advise their sons, too many executives advise their junior managers, and too many financially wealthy mentors advise young minds that to be really wealthy just turn your social conscience off and the sky is the limit for how much "wealth" you may earn. Yet we foolishly destroy ourselves and those we care about with the nearsighted pursuit of wealth at the expense of destroying the terrarium called earth that we live in. What's the use of having a fancy home or taking a vacation if you don't have the conscience to enjoy it- or worse- "living" being dishonest with yourself while rejecting the reality of your actions?

America needs to be land of opportunity for all individuals where all are created equal. Our history has left groups of individuals behind and out of network. The struggle of individuals caught in these unearned undeserved and unasked for categories is the American struggle. Some from the American right of the political spectrum feel that America is an inherent white country that was designed for white skinned people- but along with the struggle of John Adams, George Washington, Thomas Jefferson- and perhaps even more so- the social struggle of Frederick Douglass is what America is really about- Medgar Evers is what America is about- Thurgood Marshall is what America is about. If America is about the struggle for individual freedom from oppression and the pursuit of life, liberty, and the pursuit of happiness under all men are created equal- then the black skinned, brown skinned, female, homosexual, religiously (or atheist) persecuted individual struggle is what America is all about- the struggle and eventual triumph to be regarded and respected and empathized with as an equal individual in society along with everyone else- no more and no less. If it takes a shake-up of an established elitist comfortable majority culture to make this happen then so be it- it is the American thing to do.

We cannot, and should not, be able to tell who an American is by what they look like, by what music they listen to, what TV shows they watch or don't watch, the type of cars they drive, if they choose among friends to speak Spanish, or Arabic, or German, what church, mosque, or temple they choose to worship at, if they are an atheist or agnostic, etc.

Religion

The first, and preeminent, law binding point our founding fathers wanted to make was that we were not inherently a country of any particular religion- not inherently Christian or Muslim or Jewish etc. but we should enjoy the free exercise of any religion as long as it was being practiced with individual respect- inside and outside of that religion. This First Amendment prevents majority rule scenarios where if any religion had voting power of like-minded numbers of people then the individuals who were not part of that group would still be free to thrive while letting new and different ideas sift through and refresh our culture of fellow free individual people. In a majority rule society people spend the majority of their lives trying to fit in and conform to perceived cultural ideals on cultural autopilot rather than recognizing, accepting and sharing their unique individual perspectives with others. The worst-case scenario is when you have a whole society drugged under the influence of cultural conformity which lays the groundwork for a controller- in charge- above them. This could be a type of religion, or tradition, or simply stubborn cultural norms where individual expression is discouraged. This could be a version of conservatism or liberalism- on a smaller scale this could even be a family if that family inhibits the individuals within it too much beyond their ability to live, thrive, and grow, and fulfill their potential as human beings. As responsible adults we need to have a healthy sense of resistance to- and question- what we feel our culture is telling us to do automatically- without question.

NINE

From the Left

Systems are important in the lives of individuals- but are no match for individual initiative and personal accountability, and will never be alive as individuals are to bring life, love, production, thought, and peace in to the terrarium that we inhabit together.

An argument from many on the left is really the same as the case from the right- overgeneralizing individuals with white skin- particularly white males- as inherently a member of a permanent separate group from the disadvantaged non-white everybody else. In reality- a person of color and Christopher Columbus, George Armstrong Custer, and Ronald Reagan are literally in blood distant family members. *Your* ancestors, *our* ancestors- are *their* ancestors. My ancestors- and their ancestors- had black skin like yours. According to your DNA, you had ancestors in common with contemporary white people 60,000 years ago long, long, before you or your ancestors were Native American or Bantu or Muslim or were anywhere near the North American continent. The false premise currently believed by so many on the Left and Right that there is an inherent fundamental permanent group that is "white people" and then there is "everyone else" needs to go away to stop being a self-fulfilling prophecy. We are all individuals together primarily socially- and this condition we all share should be no threat to our membership in culture, religion, nation, tribe or anything else so long that they are not individually dis-respective.

The 1960's and 70's baby boomer revolution against the Vietnam war, discrimination against women, and the Archie Bunker type attitudes of many of their parents was catalytic to moving society forward a bit for individual people, but this has evolved in many cases into a dogma with too much emphasis on women's power rather than power to valid individual people who are discriminated against because they are women- black power rather than power to individual people who are discriminated against because they are black- and propped up the wrong and unjust idea that there are inherently white people and inherently black or brown people etc. Younger generations could be ready for a new- and more effective- approach towards a more open society. Young, valid, individual people may not want to be patronized, compartmentalized, overgeneralized and limited to being women, black, white, brown, gay, straight, blind, deaf, or autistic, separatists. They can recognize the unique individual person behind the skin color or gender of anyone and are bright enough not to overgeneralize and rush to judge every over 50 white male person or Utah resident they encounter. They don't have to dislike anyone automatically who is not part of an unfavored social demographic- they would love- and are ready for- a social world where they are free to interact with, respect, learn from, and love anyone they like- and yes- they can do this while bravely confronting the injustices of racial, gender, and other forms of discrimination. It's bad enough to have bigots and racists assume the ridiculous premise that individual people are fundamentally black, white, brown, female, male, etc. without liberal college professors and authors relying on the same premises.

We are each meaningfully linked even beyond the incredibly powerful bonds of our shared esoteric group experience. We don't live in a world fundamentally of systems that carry us and all others down multi-dimensional social conveyor belts. Systems are important in the lives of individuals- but are no match for individual initiative, personal accountability, and will never be alive as individuals are to bring life, love, production, thought, and peace into the terrarium that we inhabit together. No oppressive system has ever overcome the individual human spirit in the long run indefinitely. Every single life has beauty- a uniqueness and validity- and is worthy of a basic human respect along with empathy and reciprocity. Without the concept of the individual there can be no love, no empathy, no reciprocity, no respect, and no reverence. Love needs an other- someone different to illuminate ourselves and each other through sharing our differences together. It is cultural autopilot- playing a role of imitating perceived cultural ideals- that most often leads to separation of human beings while individual respect is all inclusive. It is much more lonely being in a room among people pretending to be something they are not than with only one person honestly sharing with you who they really are.

The phrase "all men are created equal" was- and is- not a white statement for white people- it is an aspirational statement of an ideal by which the individuals who codified it understood that it encompassed a reality beyond the scope of their present biases and behavior. There is no excuse in the 21st century for anything less than All people are created equal in terms of the validity and individual respect that should be afforded each and every human being. You and I are fundamentally valid individual people socially and deserve to be respected just as anyone else- no more and no less- regardless of if we have black, or brown, or white skin or are female or male- deaf or blind, homosexual or straight or transgender. We should never forget that what we look like is a very small part of the possibility and potential of who we (and all others) are. If we lose sight of our fundamental individual selves socially we can never improve who we are, the plight of our disparate groups, or our world. We are not fundamentally intrinsically- and by definition- white, black, female, Latina, Asian, homosexual, deaf, blind or anything else socially other than an individual that should be free and treated equally alongside other fellow individual people. America is not inherently 76% white, 13% black, 18% Hispanic, 6% Asian, and 2.09% Native American- America is inherently 100% fellow individual people.

The only solution to discrimination against skin color or gender is to respect people individually. If we find ourselves discriminated against because we have black or brown skin in a white skin dominated society- or because we are female in a male dominated society- our best line of defense is not to argue that we should be respected as intrinsically black, brown, or female- but rather that our skin color or gender should be irrelevant to individual respect. As repulsive as it may seem at the time of discrimination to identify with- and establish some commonality with- the jerk that is persecuting you- to rely on the honest fact that both of you are fundamentally individuals and that you deserve the same basic human individual respect that he does defeats his weak reasoned argument that somehow white skin is superior to black- or that men are superior to women. In an election environment where a majority is white skinned and male and the majority's white skinned or male votes would be helpful quantitatively in the effort and are needed to support justice for the black or brown or female minority- those white male voters are most likely to be supportive of black, brown, or female people that they believe are fundamentally *their people* as fellow individual human beings first- rather than people they over-generalize as fundamentally black, brown, or female- and therefore intrinsically members of "the other" group.

There is only one group for which situations can be honestly judged as just or fair and it isn't white, black, or brown skinned people or male or female people- it is only individual people that justice can honestly address. All white, black, brown skinned and male or female people are valid individual people and being valid individual people among each other is their common link and their only basis of common justice. A black skinned person is unjustly treated if they are not treated as the valid individual person that they in fact are.

You cannot be credible in wanting individual respect for yourself while at the same time over generalizing others as fundamentally white, black, or brown people. It is unjust to judge or discriminate against a white skinned individual as "guilty of being white" as it is to judge or discriminate against a black skinned individual as "guilty of being black". This attitude is self-defeating because others have no way to change their skin color and their only option is to change their attitudes and behavior as individuals like yourself. You would be better served and more honest and accurate by always adding the word individuals after saying white or black or Latina or male or female etc. because then you are including them among yourself and others- we can do this and still take into consideration the particular realities of what it means to be black, brown or female etc. in America.

If we say that we know what happened in a situation among other individuals when we weren't there and automatically take the side of the individuals that are among our idea of "our people"- then it is a simple fact that we are not on the side of justice. When there is an instance of conflict between the police and a person of color- given the history and number of instances where the black or brown skinned person was treated differently than other individuals because of the color of their skin - the question must be considered- was this individual discriminated against because of their skin color? However, it is also critical for the justice of all involved that an assessment must be done determining as fairly as possible how did each individual act in the situation on an individual level. What actually did the individual police officer do? What were the exact actions of the individual who was in conflict with the police officer? Could a relative of this last individual honestly without bias identify and empathize with that police officer as a fellow individual human being, father, or husband who needs to protect their own life as well as the public in a potentially dangerous situation? Could a fellow police officer find the courage to call out and report another officer who they feel have just violated someone's individual rights- or worse murdered someone?

Please ask yourself when you are considering a conflict situation between groups do you really want justice for the individuals involved or do you have a bias in favor of the white skinned, black skinned, brown skinned, gay or straight, male or female individuals involved? Who are *your* people? We need to establish a general attitude and societal norm that gives all involved a basic individual respect.

All human beings including all white skinned human beings and all black skinned human beings and everyone else- are fundamentally indigenous and natural to our common planet Earth and are natural elements of our biological and environmental terrarium.

When schoolchildren think of "indigenous" people they may think of only brown or black skinned people. It is good to appreciate the culture and lineage of groups of people who settled certain parts of our planet before others- but we should never forget that all human beings including all white skinned human beings and all black skinned human beings and everyone else- are fundamentally indigenous and natural elements of our planet Earth. We are all, as humans, biologically related through our common DNA. We are literally blood family. Our common family ancestors originated and lived together in a relatively small part of our world before they spread over the planet and began to acquire different skin colors and languages and cultures and religions etc. In this way the ancestors of the Hopi are also the ancestors of the Norwegians as well as the Tutsi and Japanese and the Bolivians, the Greeks, the Christians, the Jews, the Muslims, the Americans, all Catholics, all Nazis, all Communists, all homosexual people, all females and males, all Mormons and Baptists. And all these groups are made up intrinsically of valid individual people like you and I who should be respected and empathized with and treated justly with reciprocity individually among all others- no more and no less- even when they are under the jurisdiction of any culture or religion.

All of the above humans need certain things- food, healthcare, housing, jobs, clean air to breathe, a functioning planetary ecosystem, etc. These things need to be either directly produced or at least facilitated by individual production- and it takes the market incentivized production of many individuals with different motivations to cooperate to make even a simple pencil- much less a smart phone (see Milton Friedman's Pencil Story). Command and control systems where the state generally controls production such as those of the USSR and China in the 20th century failed to produce these things as well as the individual exchange-based market economies of those in the west. After allowing more free market interaction among individuals China has improved its economy significantly. When we say we have a right to healthcare- we are we really saying that we have a right to force a doctor or nurse to provide it for us whether they feel adequately compensated or not- which is against individual rights (just consider the reciprocity- would you like to be forced to produce something for someone else?). A great rule of thumb for the left is to never demand that the public should have something without backing it up with how fellow individual people could make that happen. "Free food for everybody?"- great- just detail for us how that would be produced without force and how would individuals be incentivized and still have the freedom and prosperity that you personally would like to enjoy.

We should rather say that we have a desire and agreement as a community that certain limited things such as health insurance, or funding our military, or regulating our ports or food or labor safety should be done by the public sector rather than for profit businesses- because private insurance companies don't make a profit by insuring individuals with pre- existing conditions- and some businesspeople don't have a problem with hiring 8 year old kids for factory work- or degrading our climate or air quality or oceans for oil profits.

If left minded people want the state to step in in cases where private markets don't have a profit incentive to produce- such as comprehensive health insurance coverage for every citizen or enforcement of child labor laws- the funding for these programs must come from taxes paid by private businesses that are profitable enough to pay them- and the more profit the businesses make the more tax revenue they generate. So since it is business and profit that supports the desires of the left- and therefore the left, out of rational self-interest, should be supportive of business and profit. Business and profit that is inefficient or tyrannized by overly bureaucratic government systems and over-strenuous taxation will not serve their cause. The key lies in incentivizing individual people to produce economically in a way that benefits all supports the desires of the left- and therefore the left, out of rational self- interest, should be generally supportive of business and profit.

Of course, like conservatives, different people who define themselves as "Liberal" have different views on what this word means. Among the positive attitudes are a belief in human stewardship of our natural environment, protection of the rights and promoting the opportunities of the disadvantaged in society, promotion of enlightenment-based values, and a healthy promotion of the idea that, on the whole, materialism and financial greed unchecked hurt human beings in the aggregate and the rest of the flora, fauna and climate on our shared planet.

Like Conservatism, however, lurking around some corners in the back alleys among Liberal thought are some attitudes that are not individually respective. There is a notion among some self-identified Liberals that they belong to the ongoing permanent anti-establishment group (group B) against the permanent establishment group in power above them- which is the traditional white male dominated society (group A). These folks view themselves as the only legitimate alternative to Group A but they don't realize that in many ways the anti-establishment culture is almost- if not more in some ways- a strict establishment culture than the one from which they are supposedly liberated against. In some 60's circles one was cool and politically correct if one conformed to the latest clothes styles, drug choices, music choices etc. but was not considered cool or accepted if one did not. Soldiers were called names and spat upon. So Liberalism of that type- not unlike some motorcycle ad campaign- seemed to offer an individually liberating freedom alternative to a fixed permanent establishment culture-but often was something individuals went to actually to conform to a perception of being cool in the eyes of some socially ideal group they imagine is judging them approvingly.

There's been a fair amount of social conformity placed above the common sharing of individual enlightenment in Liberalism. Of course, against a regime you need groups to mobilize together against a common enemy- you need some cohesion. Quantitative force of numbers is everything in a battle for change within a democracy- but this partitioning of groups too often leads to factions who believe that they are permanently separate from each other and momentum towards a socially dysfunctional pluralistic future world of separated silo tribes who won't engage, share, and learn from each other individually.

Again, we should ask ourselves: 1. Do we want to be regarded and respected generally as unique individuals by others or do we want to be judged principally and over-generalized by the color of our skin, gender, religious affiliation, nationality, cultural association, or physical challenge? 2. What steps are necessary for that reality to happen generally for you personally and all your fellow individual human beings? 3. Is the path you are taking individually and socially following those steps that lead to that conclusion? Are the steps you are taking now leading away from that conclusion? If the answer to number one above is yes-then: No it is not right or just to automatically dislike a stranger we have never met if it is said that they have white skin, are a police officer, are a member of a certain religion, live in a "red" state, wear clothes we don't like etc. We have no idea who these individuals are or what their potential is- or what their attitudes (or their children's attitudes) could be in the future.

We will never have a just and free society when there is too much emphasis on protecting culture and not enough on respecting and fostering individuals among the populace. Since feudalism and the evolution of markets individual people have more freely exchanged ideas and production together and have thus created the greatest material quality of life and *subversion of establishment* for more people in the history of humanity-much more than socialism, or communism, or dictatorship etc. We need to make our jobs and attitudes more friendly to our planet and each other and we can socially evolve to be a more beneficial part of our natural ecosystem together.

Would you benefit as a person of color if we lived in a world of individual respect? Would your grandchildren benefit from that world? How are we going to get there? What is the process?

TEN

///

Religion

We must honestly begin with ourselves as individuals before we can relate to any, and all, religion. We are each born blank slates without knowledge of the world around us. We came into this world individually not as Christians or Muslims or Hindus but learned about religion and culture from our social environment. Religion requires our individual honesty towards it for reverence- and honesty requires earnest self-examination and introspection. We are born individuals before we learn about any religion- and most religions require, and thus value, our eventual individual participation, belief, consent or submission- because, as adults, we are not automatically enrolled, and are unable to be honestly reverent, in any religion without our earnest individual engagement.

Among the major components of human social reality are individuals, ideals, attitudes and behaviors. Most human beings agree that they did not biologically create themselves and those they love and care about and their natural environment- that there are seemingly transcendent ideals like goodness, fairness, good fortune or bad fortune (life patterns just seemingly going our way or not for short periods of time) that seem to exist beyond our overt direction or control. Many perceive and feel comfortable with a transcendent supreme creator, authority, source of all goodness that they should submit to in order to be consistent and properly reverent in the natural harmony of the cosmos. God for many is an ideal in being form but also an individual. Others believe that we are all children of nature with science as our source of information about the mysteries of existence. Still others may feel that they should direct themselves and do not believe in the existence of any transcendent power at all. We shouldn't kill or punish people for exploring, learning, wrestling with their conscience, and deciding for themselves on these things. These are tough decisions for people coming from different perspectives. People with these differing beliefs and attitudes should be free to live together, share and discuss their points of view, and perhaps even argue and disagree- without harming or killing each other.

Religion has no problem with self-recognition, empathy, and reciprocity or the 3 questions:

1. Do you want to be regarded and respected generally as a unique individual by others or do you want to be judged principally and over-generalized by the color of your skin, gender, religious affiliation, nationality, cultural association, or physical challenge?

2. What steps are necessary for that reality to happen generally for you and all your fellow individual human beings?

3. Is the path you are taking individually and socially following those steps that lead to that conclusion?

We can still be absolutely reverent to our religions as long as they don't stand in the way of, obscure, or subvert, a basic individual respect and priority of basic human rights between ourselves as fellow individual people sharing the same planet together. Our religious belief need not have any restrictions socially but only in religious *practice- if that practice violates the individual rights of others.* You and everyone else benefits with individual respect concerning behavior between individuals of different religions.

Unfortunately, there are those who are devout believers of Christianity, Judaism, Islam, and other religions who are not living as socially good behaving people towards others in reference to individual respect, empathy and reciprocity.

A major problem (perhaps THE major social problem) among humans is when they buy into the belief that they are not connected to all humans but that they are fundamentally members of separate groups- and religion- in the past and present- has unfortunately, been a means for that. No religion separates us fundamentally from other human beings at the 'fellow individuals in context' social level. We cannot let culture or religion divide us from our other fellow individual human beings- it is one of the things that can fool us into believing that there are inherent static groups of people in our world- which is not true.

Religions can have a bad influence if they downplay an individual's personal accountability. We as individuals are always personally accountable among ALL others for our behavior. If I stole the banana no one else did- I did- and although why I stole the banana should be taken into consideration upon judging me- this can never remove the factual reality that I stole the banana. A religion should not say that it is natural that I stole the banana (and to continue stealing bananas) and my only redemption from that act relies on turning myself over to that particular religion (and by the way I am cleared from wrongdoing in such acts in the future as long as I am repentant to the religion.) Unfortunately, there are way too many businesspeople who rationalize and justify their consistent bad behavior in the business world on Mondays by relying on their mantle of righteousness on Sundays.

Religion can have a bad influence on people if it encourages cultural autopilot and removes the sense of individual introspection, self-examination, and the desire to thoughtfully examine and question reality around oneself. Too many turn to religion with the attitude of "If I could just hand my individual self over to this particular culture of religion I would be alright and have social warmth and community and not have to make decisions about directing my life according to conscience."- religion is this to many people. Some actually lose their individual selves to these pre-packaged waves of thought. In this way many have lost their connection to their God who would desire them to be open-eyed and intentionally reverent- to charlatan "church leaders" who gain power by directing sheep who won't think for themselves. One can still "hand oneself over" to a religion and still maintain their individuality (that surely their God created for a reason), as well as their sense of basic community with- and responsibility towards- their fellow human beings.

ELEVEN

///

The United States of America

The foundation of the ideal of The United States of America starts with the Declaration of Independence- in this are the definitive American ideals- our national creed - foremost is the principle that all men are created equal- meaning all human beings everywhere- globally- have a basic agency and validity and are due a basic individual respect, empathy, and reciprocity underneath their cultures, religions, nationalities, skin color, gender, etc. This involves a belief and attitude that that person across the world is fundamentally socially one of your fellow human beings first and foremost- before they are an Afghan or Muslim or Christian or Russian or North Korean etc. This requires introspection, honesty, confidence and courage to accept this reality and to adopt this attitude (by the way this is the view of Jesus of Nazareth- of Mohamed- of Buddha- of Shakespeare- of The Enlightenment- none of these would support the view that culture or skin color inherently defined human beings apart from other perceived groups of people). There is nothing American about looking at one's skin color or religion or culture and believing this is what America should be about- America is for the individual in all of us at the individual base level we all share in common before we get to the cultural, racial, gender, religious, or sexual orientation attributes we have that may separate us culturally. If we don't have general and sincere individual respect among ourselves as citizens we don't have a USA. We are individuals among each other first before we are members of any culture, religion, race, gender, or sexual orientation and we emphasize and exercise a profound individual respect and tolerance as an essential part of our national creed. Case in point if our American founders intended us to be a designated Christian country they would have said so- instead they went to great lengths to make clear their intention in the very 1st amendment- free exercise of any religion but no particular state religion. We can certainly choose to be and act wholeheartedly Christian, Muslim, or Jewish- but we are not a Christian, Muslim, or Jewish governed nation.

Our country was designed for one particular group of people in mind- individual persons- a group which includes and encompasses all people, regardless of what they look like or who- or if- they worship, underneath and across any category of race, ethnicity, gender, religion, tribe, or culture. Our country was not designed specifically for white skinned people- or Christians, or any culture in particular- except a culture of individual respect- or at the very least a basic tolerance- between people. An original founding American ideal was the inclusion of fellow human beings from anywhere on our planet who were welcome to bring their religious or cultural beliefs with them so long as respect for the individual and the rule of law should be prioritized should religious or cultural practice come into conflict with that basic individual respect or rule of law. If you are Christian, Muslim, Jewish, Hindu, Buddhist, Atheist or Agnostic it is literally the American way that you be welcome here- but should you share your religion with large numbers of other people in America- you will never be respected and honored by law as America's National Religion- your religion will always be subject to a practice of basic individual respect towards all others and the rule of law in this country- and you cannot obstruct the free exercise of other religions (with their same caveat regarding individual respect and the rule of law). This idea was the first and number one priority of our founding fathers in their vision for the relationship between individual citizens and their government when establishing this country.

How does conservatism measure up to American Ideals? Consider the following quotes:

> "*Congress shall make no law respecting an establishment of religion, or prohibiting the free exercise thereof*" - The United States Constitution

"The bosom of America is open to receive not only the opulent & respectable Stranger, but the oppressed & persecuted of all Nations & Religions; whom we shall wellcome to a participation of all our rights & previleges, if by decency & propriety of conduct they appear to merit the enjoyment."

– George Washington to Joshua Holmes, 2 December 1783

"… neither Pagan nor Mahomedan nor Jew ought to be excluded from the civil rights of the Commonwealth because of his religion." – Thomas Jefferson

"As the Government of the United States of America is not, in any sense, founded on the Christian religion; as it has in itself no character of enmity against the laws, religion, or tranquillity, of Mussulmen; and, as the said States never entered into any war, or act of hostility against any Mahometan nation, it is declared by the parties, that no pretext arising from religious opinions, shall ever produce an interruption of the harmony existing between the two countries." – Treaty of Tripoli (1796), signed by President John Adams

"We ought to consider what is the end of government, before we determine which is the best form. Upon this point all speculative politicians will agree, that the happiness of society is the end of government, as all Divines and moral Philosophers will agree that the happiness of the individual is the end of man. From this principle it will follow, that the form of government which communicates ease, comfort, security, or, in one word, happiness, to the greatest number of persons, and in the greatest degree, is the best." -John Adams

"The prevailing ideas entertained by [Jefferson] and most of the leading statesmen at the time of the formation of the old constitution, were that the enslavement of the African was in violation of the laws of nature; that it was wrong in

principle, socially, morally, and politically. It was an evil they knew not well how to deal with, but the general opinion of the men of that day was that, somehow or other in the order of Providence, the institution would be evanescent and pass away. This idea, though not incorporated in the constitution, was the prevailing idea at that time. The constitution, it is true, secured every essential guarantee to the institution while it should last, and hence no argument can be justly urged against the constitutional guarantees thus secured, because of the common sentiment of the day. Those ideas, however, were fundamentally wrong. They rested upon the assumption of the equality of races. This was an error. It was a sandy foundation, and the government built upon it fell when the "storm came and the wind blew."

"Our new government is founded upon exactly the opposite idea; its foundations are laid, its corner-stone rests, upon the great truth that the negro is not equal to the white man; that slavery subordination to the superior race is his natural and normal condition. This, our new government, is the first, in the history of the world, based upon this great physical, philosophical, and moral truth."

- Confederate Alexander Stephens from Cornerstone speech

"We have a civil religion in this country. He (Thomas Jefferson) provided our catechism. No one knows how to become French. We know when we started July 4 1776 and we know how we become an American- you come here and you assent- then you're an American. You're in- you're it- just as American as anybody who's family has been here for 10 generations"

- George Will from Ken Burn's Thomas Jefferson

"You know that nobody wishes more ardently to see an abolition not only of the trade but of the condition of slavery:

and certainly nobody will be more willing to encounter every sacrifice for that object." -Thomas Jefferson to Brissot de Warville, February 11, 1788

"God grant, that not only the Love of Liberty, but a thorough knowledge of the Rights of Man, may pervade all the Nations of the Earth, so that a Philosopher may set his Foot Anywhere on its Surface, and say, 'This is my Country.'"- Benjamin Franklin 1789

"All sober inquirers after truth, ancient and modern, pagan and Christian, have declared that the happiness of man, as well as his dignity, consists in virtue. Confucius, Zo-roaster, Socrates, Mahomet, not to mention authorities really sacred, have agreed in this." – "Thoughts on Government" by President John Adams

"I think certainly if you are an African American, slavery is at the center of what you see as the American experience. But, for most Americans, most of the time, there were a lot of other things going on."

-Newt Gingrich August 19, 2019 Fox News

"The story of the negro in America IS the story of America- and it is not a pretty story."- James Baldwin

Conservatism is one of the great waves of thought that individual people are born into, jump into or fall into and often don't get out of- but all conservatives are individuals first and foremost among all other people and conservatism, or liberalism, or any other "ism", shouldn't erode the reality that individual respect, empathy, and reciprocity are every human being's inherent natural moral values before any cultural or systemic obligations. We humans are all born with an individual obligation to treat all others with a primary individual respect and reciprocity- regardless if they belong to a group we belong to or not- such as skin color, gender, culture, language, religion, nationality, sexual orientation, etc. We are behaving morally if we do this- we are not behaving morally if we do not.

Our country's Declaration of course begins:

"In Congress, July 4, 1776.

    The unanimous Declaration of the thirteen united States of America, When in the Course of human events, it becomes necessary for one people to dissolve the political bands which have connected them with another, and to assume among the powers of the earth, the separate and equal station to which the Laws of Nature and of Nature's God entitle them, a decent respect to the opinions of mankind requires that they should declare the causes which impel them to the separation.

    We hold these truths to be self-evident, that all men are created equal, that they are endowed by their Creator with certain unalienable Rights, that among these are Life, Liberty and the pursuit of Happiness.—That to secure these rights, Governments are instituted among Men, deriving their just powers from the consent of the governed, —That whenever any Form of Government becomes destructive of these ends, it is the Right of the People to alter or to abolish it, and to institute new Government, laying its foundation on such principles and organizing its powers in such form, as to them shall seem most likely to effect their Safety and Happiness."

The Preamble of our constitution begins:

We the People of the United States, in Order to form a more perfect Union, establish Justice, insure domestic Tranquility, provide for the common defence, promote the general Welfare, and secure the Blessings of Liberty to ourselves and our Posterity, do ordain and establish this Constitution for the United States of America.

Joe McNeill

Our bill of rights is as follows:

> *Amendment I Congress shall make no law respecting an establishment of religion, or prohibiting the free exercise thereof; or abridging the freedom of speech, or of the press; or the right of the people peaceably to assemble, and to petition the Government for a redress of grievances.*
>
> *Amendment II A well regulated Militia, being necessary to the security of a free State, the right of the people to keep and bear Arms, shall not be infringed.*
>
> *Amendment III No Soldier shall, in time of peace be quartered in any house, without the consent of the Owner, nor in time of war, but in a manner to be prescribed by law.*
>
> *Amendment IV The right of the people to be secure in their persons, houses, papers, and effects, against unreasonable searches and seizures, shall not be violated, and no Warrants shall issue, but upon probable cause, supported by Oath or affirmation, and particularly describing the place to be searched, and the persons or things to be seized.*
>
> *Amendment V No person shall be held to answer for a capital, or otherwise infamous crime, unless on a presentment or indictment of a Grand Jury, except in cases arising in the land or naval forces, or in the Militia, when in actual service in time of War or public danger; nor shall any person be subject for the same offence to be twice put in jeopardy of life or limb; nor shall be compelled in any criminal case to be a witness against himself, nor be deprived of life, liberty, or property, without due process of law; nor shall private property be taken for public use, without just compensation.*
>
> *Amendment VI In all criminal prosecutions, the accused shall enjoy the right to a speedy and public trial, by an impartial jury of the State and district wherein the crime*

shall have been committed, which district shall have been previously ascertained by law, and to be informed of the nature and cause of the accusation; to be confronted with the witnesses against him; to have compulsory process for obtaining witnesses in his favor, and to have the Assistance of Counsel for his defence.

Amendment VII In Suits at common law, where the value in controversy shall exceed twenty dollars, the right of trial by jury shall be preserved, and no fact tried by a jury, shall be otherwise re-examined in any Court of the United States, than according to the rules of the common law.

Amendment VIII Excessive bail shall not be required, nor excessive fines imposed, nor cruel and unusual punishments inflicted.

Amendment IX The enumeration in the Constitution, of certain rights, shall not be construed to deny or disparage others retained by the people.

Amendment X The powers not delegated to the United States by the Constitution, nor prohibited by it to the States, are reserved to the States respectively, or to the people.

From the above a reasonable person may infer that- in America:

- Ideals of Individual rights among people should be prioritized above any cultural or even religious practice that may subjugate individual rights.
- That our govt is not to champion any one religion over another- that there is certainly no national religion
- That we are certainly not a country where the norms of a particular culture or religion are to be propped up in any way by our government as the establishment.

- That all people including any race or gender are due a basic individual respect and individual rights as any other-equal in spirit and practice and before the law.
- That we have never been isolationist in nature but felt ourselves connected to and inherently integrated as a part of the rest of our world and that all other fellow individuals are linked to us fundamentally as our fellow mankind wherever they might be.
- There is nothing in the founding ideals that suggests that there is a patriotism in protecting a particular culture but in fact individual freedom is emphasized, prioritized and codified in the face of social structure and even religion.

It was the ideals that mattered. Our founding fathers laid out the ideals for a great America and a great planet and though we have fallen short in practice we should keep our aspirations on those ideals.

TWELVE

///

Our Future Together

H opefully in the near future our children will be raised by parents who place a high priority on individual respect and personal accountability- go to schools where they are given equal individual respect, treatment, curriculum and care regardless of their skin color, gender, physical challenge, sexual orientation, or religious (or non-religious) background- and work in businesses where they are honestly respected and judged only individually and not discriminated against because of attributes they have that are not relevant to their job. They will aspire the best they can to be themselves rather than live their lives on cultural autopilot with the sole (soul) ambition of conforming to, and imitating, cultural ideals and cliches.

They will be free to choose any religion or non-religion according to their own conscience- be socially comfortable in their skin color, gender, sexual orientation, or physical challenge- be free to question anything (culture, religion, teaching, government or movement) that they choose. They will not make social demands such as "free widgets for everybody" without examining and understanding how those demands would be produced and how those producing them would be justly compensated. They would not believe in the existence of permanent establishments above them that, in their view, should take care of or provide for everyone- but-in their view- are inherently bad so they don't. They will believe that generally if they want something for themselves or someone else then they should produce it themselves or persuade others to voluntarily get onboard to produce that outcome.

When they encounter another person, even a stranger, they will see an individual person like themselves first and not a skin color, or gender, or religion, or culture, or language, or nationality first- and relate to that person- almost automatically- with individual respect, empathy and reciprocity.

They will view themselves and all others here as natural lifeforms of this shared planet existing with other species and will strive to foster- and not detract from- the natural terrarium (and the included flora and fauna around them) which is their home.

In a world of conflict between groups who have continually advancing weapons of mass destruction and where world-wide cooperation is needed to solve problems such as social oppression, sustainable energy, pollution, food distribution and climate change- we must have these people- we must have these attitudes for communication, understanding, and problem solving. We are out of time.

CITATIONS

1. Blow, Charles M. The Devil You Know: A Black Power Manifesto (2021). Harper
2. Wikipedia The Free Encyclopedia, Conservatism in the United States

Printed in the United States
by Baker & Taylor Publisher Services